THREE
ENGLISH WOMEN
IN AMERICA

The three women of the title, Fanny Trollope, Fanny Kemble and Harriet Martineau, visited or made their homes in the United States between 1826 and 1836. Three very different personalities, they all left lively records of their American experiences, which are described with wit and warmth by Una Pope-Hennessy.

The most eccentric of the three was Fanny Trollope, the mother of the famed British novelist, who wrote no less than 115 books before her death in 1863; Fanny Kemble was the niece of the great actress, Sarah Siddons, and lived in America only while enduring an unsuccessful marriage; Harriet Martineau was a formidable blue stocking, with a tendency to climb all famous monuments!

First published in 1929, *Three English Women in America* also provides a unique comparative study of life for women in nineteenth century America, by the author of *Maxims of a Queen, Secret Societies and the French Revolution* and *Madame Roland.*

Also in the Century Travellers

On Sledge and Horseback to Outcast Siberian Lepers by Kate Marsden
Introduction by Eric Newby

East is West by Freya Stark

The Waiting Land by Dervla Murphy

Every Rock, Every Hill by Victoria Schofield

A Sabine Journey by Anthony Rhodes
Introduction by Peter Quennell

The Rivers Amazon by Alex Shoumatoff

The Island by Anton Chekhov
Introduction by Irina Ratushinskaya

In Morocco by Edith Wharton

Uttermost Part of the Earth by Lucas Bridges
Introduction by Gavin Young

Life in Mexico by Madame Calderon de la Barca
Introduction by Sir Nicolas Cheetham

Touring in 1600 by E.S. Bates
Introduction by George Bull

A Pilgrimage to Nejd by Lady Anne Blunt

Coups and Cocaine by Anthony Daniels

THREE ENGLISH WOMEN IN AMERICA

Una Pope-Hennessy

Century
London Melbourne Auckland Johannesburg

First published in 1929 by Ernest Benn Ltd

© Estate of Una Pope-Hennessy 1987

This edition first published in 1987 by Century, an imprint of
Century Hutchinson Ltd,
Brookmount House, 62–65 Chandos Place, London
WC2N 4NW

Century Hutchinson Australia Pty Ltd
PO Box 495, 16–22 Church Street, Hawthorn, Victoria 3122,
Australia

Century Hutchinson New Zealand Limited
PO Box 40-086, Glenfield, Auckland 10, New Zealand

Century Hutchinson South Africa (Pty) Ltd
PO Box 337, Berglvei, 2012 South Africa

ISBN 0 7126 1792 2

Printed in Great Britain by,
Richard Clay Ltd, Bungay, Suffolk

To
R. P-H.
J.W. P-H.
R.J. P-H.
In memory of happy days spent
together in Massachusetts.

CONTENTS

INTRODUCTION   *Page* 13

FANNY TROLLOPE   *page* 23

   With a portrait of FANNY TROLLOPE *by Auguste Hervieu*   32

FANNY KEMBLE   *page* 113

   With a portrait of FANNY KEMBLE *by Sir Thomas Lawrence*   122

   and a portrait by Thomas Sully   200

HARRIET MARTINEAU   *page* 211

   With a portrait of HARRIET MARTINEAU *by R. Evans*   236

   and a portrait by C. Osgood   282

INTRODUCTION

INTRODUCTION

A CENTURY ago the country known to travellers as the United States was about one-third of its present size, with the Mississippi forming a wild western frontier. The Atlantic could be traversed by sailing-ship in from three to six weeks, but in spite of long intercourse with Europe and the existence of old cultural centres in New England, Pennsylvania, and Virginia, the country itself was still in an uncivilized condition. Indiana and Illinois were sparsely settled; Chicago was a village of about twenty houses; Detroit a hamlet. The west bank of the Mississippi had few colonists save in Louisiana, which was parcelled out into cotton fields and sugar plantations. Nine million free citizens and two million slaves inhabited the vast areas of the States and Territories.

Sitting down with a map spread out before him, a prospective tourist would at once grasp the fact that the easiest places to get at were those attainable by water transport. From New York, for example, it was possible to steam up the Hudson to Albany and thence to pierce farther inland by the Erie Canal and embark on the Great Lakes. Then again, it was easy to take ship from New York to Providence, and jolting thence to Boston by road, to investigate the industrial towns of New England. A journey through the Southern

States was fraught with more difficulties, for it was necessary either to coast along with many changes and delays from seaport to seaport or to travel by stage. Old calendars, road books, and gazetteers show what an immense and fatiguing undertaking it was to drive from point to point in America. Southern gentlemen returning to their plantations from Philadelphia had been seen to crumple up completely from exhaustion after a week of such travelling, despite the cool mint-juleps tendered to them at each halt.

The slave States occupied about two-thirds of the area of the United States and presented an irresistible lure for Europeans. With feelings compounded of curiosity, repugnance, and sentimentality they plunged into Virginia, easing themselves into a kind of acquiescence in conditions which theoretically they abhorred, when they saw the beaming negro in aristocratic houses and stables. Pressing on by the James River to the coast or by stage through the Carolinas, they tasted the full flavour of the South amidst the toilers in the swamps of Georgia and the plantations of Alabama. Embarking at New Orleans they were able to complete their circular tour by mounting the great rivers and landing at Pittsburgh.

No decade in American history is more pregnant with development than that between 1826 and 1836. The first of the three women travellers whose adventures are described in this book never boarded a train, because in her day there were none; the last, nine years later, rode in one a distance of eighty-one miles in seven hours. True, that thirteen holes were burnt in her dress by flying cinders and her veil destroyed, but that was only to be expected in such a novel and pleasant form of locomotion.

All travellers of that day speak much of the prevalent sicknesses and the unhealthiness of the country, but we must remember it takes a long time to subjugate nature. That alone can be done by draining marshes, building shelters against extremes of cold and heat, destroying insects and distributing wholesome food. The oozy rice-fields of the Carolinas, the cotton areas of Alabama, the sugar brakes of Louisiana were all in their seasons conducive to fever and deadly. Except in market towns the food was poor and scanty. A traveller could expect nothing at a wayside inn but dried venison or ham, milkless tea and sour bread. Occasionally a chicken would be caught and broiled and a head of maize cooked, but for the most part the fare was primitive and dull. The vagaries of climate and temperature were much as they are to-day, when the rains and fogs of New England set off the steamy haze of the Mississippi delta.

Harriet Martineau was the only one of the three women who set out to interpret America from what she believed to be the American point of view, and she began by clearing her mind of the besetting sin of comparison. Before she sailed a London publisher tried to buy her opinions in advance for four hundred pounds. When she returned home the bidding was raised by several firms and culminated in an offer of two thousand pounds. That is a measure of the desire of people in England to obtain a fair, rational account of American civilization. Mrs. Trollope's book was widely read on both sides of the ocean and is reported to have brought her in some nine hundred pounds. Among publishers in London it gave life to a new verb, "to trollopise", meaning to sermonise on experiences. In America when a man threw his legs on a balcony or spat on the floor of a music-hall he heard shouts of "a trollope! a trollope!" People in saloons and stores and places of amusement became rapidly familiar with Mrs. Trollope's strictures on American manners.

No English persons of that day were ever prepared to admit that they were not generally attractive and superior to every foreigner they met. Further, they came to America with the delusion that a common language involved a common understanding, and since they were the owners and creators of that language they felt free to laugh at Yankee pronunciation and intonation. It was always a shock to English people to find not only that they were not more welcome than French or Germans, but that the memory of Lafayette, Steuben, and Kosciusko was deeply venerated, and that no English names were honoured in the same way. A courteous but nationally impartial welcome awaited all persons of distinction; indeed, owing to the truly American instinct for paying homage where homage is due, many foreigners were, in the language of that day, "lafayetted".

There were obvious reasons why English people
should be less liked than continental people, for the
traditions of the War of Independence and the vivid
stories of the war which had closed twelve years previously gave most American men and women a subsoil
of antipathy in the make-up of their minds, just as the
underlining in children's school-books to-day of the
grievances set forth in the Declaration of Independence
to some extent prejudices them when actual contacts
take place. Personal relations in the case of Harriet
Martineau and Fanny Kemble cemented close friendships, and the general kindliness of American hearts
made most intercourse pleasant save with the pioneers
and democrats of the West. They were rough and
gloried in their tobacco-chewing, their spitting, their
whisky, and their torrid oaths. When these people
came to Washington to support President Jackson,
the silk-stockinged, knee-breeched parties of the White
House were invaded by the tousled heads and home-
spun coats of farmers and river men. Just as surely as
the salons of Paris were destined to be blotted out by
the Jacobins of the Revolution, so did this infiltration
portend the knell of European influence in Washington.
The rise of the sovereign people, unpleasant as it may
be for those who sit on the thrones of privilege and
tradition, has in it something of the order of a sup-
pressed natural force, a welling up of life that is
irresistible.

President Jackson, whose terms of office synchron-
ized with the visits of these English women, symbolized

17

the break with Europe. Henceforth, America was to be America and sink or swim of her own genius. A sort of instinct made manifest that for generations to come the pioneer interest must be paramount and the whole energy and grit of the nation turned into the channel of getting the country going and the ground subjugated. A great output of will to conquer forests, floods, beasts, Indians, to wring a destiny out of nature, made attention to the European fandangle known as "culture" a waste of time. Unconsciously and by force of circumstances the Americans became a nomad people and the heritage of this decisive moment is woven into the texture of their present life. Westward lay their appointed way: in the West their sun was rising: to that sun's warm rays they opened their hearts.

Looking forth from a balloon in those days one would have seen ant-like processions of waggons and men and animals on every track from the East to the West and the South. The pioneers were moving in pursuit of a vision. Much to be done and life very short. Rainbow prospects across rivers in worlds without end. The trekkers taught their children that independence was a great good, that they had done with old European ideas of vassalage and entered into a new freedom. The radiant dream was an intoxication to men whose fathers and forefathers had maintained the station in life to which it had pleased God to call them. No master and no man, a life of boundless opportunity, land for the taking, wealth for the working; no frontier and no foreigner. Freedom to work in manly independence alone with nature and with comrades. Could any man ask more?

In this pulsating decade of its history three unusually intelligent English women precipitated themselves into American life. Their experiences were widely different, and all dived well below the surface of society. By their stories something of America may be known.

FANNY TROLLOPE

FANNY TROLLOPE

§ I

No English name has been held in greater execration among Americans than that of Fanny Trollope. Setting out in the reign of George IV. to trade in knick-knacks with the simple inhabitants of the New World, much as in the old days people sailed for the West Coast of Africa to exchange beads and buttons for ivory and gold, she met with experiences so unexpected as to appear to her to be worthy of record. The record shaped itself into an attack on the habits, manners, and education of the American people, the decadence of which she came to attribute to the prevalence among them of nonsensical democratic notions of equality. Time has to some degree dulled the pungency of her onslaught, nevertheless the Trollope tradition is woven into the impalpable veil that hangs between English and American minds and makes them inscrutable to each other yet.

For an English woman, accompanied by three children, to seek her fortune beyond the ocean was a century ago a bold venture. And even to-day the more one considers Mrs. Trollope's procedure, the more it assumes the complexion of temerity. To break up home and family in England and trust herself to carry out an enterprise for which no previous experience had fitted her was rash enough, but to drag three half-grown children across the world with her was positively reckless. However, being a sanguine, competent woman, accustomed to having her own way, she saw nothing she did not wish to see, thereby sharing the temperament of those Englishmen who have lightly added a province to the Empire or have died philosophically in some remote zareba.

It must not be supposed that Mrs. Trollope was consciously prejudiced against the ideas of equality or democracy before she left home. Rather the contrary was the case, for the accounts of the American Commonwealth, in so far as it seemed to embody the vague liberal, half-communist aspirations of political refugee acquaintances and radical friends, filled her mind with attractive pictures of a simpler England "broad based upon a people's will". Perhaps it was because she envisaged America as her own country over again with all its faults and injustices eliminated that the decision to cross the Atlantic was taken without apparent misgiving. The assumption that any mitigation of the austere fraternal life lived in the land of liberty must be acceptable, inspired her to prepare to supply its denizens with up-to-date luxuries—pincushions, watch-guards, pen-knives, Tonbridge ware, pepper-casters, toilet-table ornaments—such as graced the new bazaars of Oxford Street. Once an idea had got into Mrs. Trollope's head, it was almost impossible to get it out again, and it is doubtful whether the humorous conviction that pioneers should be provided with fancy goods was dislodged even by the galling rebuffs that attended the prosecution of her plan. Enthusiastic friends like Frances Wright and General Lafayette had so inflated her with gaseous theories that she believed America to be a paradise where everyone was noble-minded and kind and no one was downtrodden or poor. No risk, therefore, was associated in her mind with taking children to such an Elysium. Like many optimistic people she ignored trouble until it tripped her up, for she could rely on her health, good temper, and sense of superiority to triumph over most accidents and emergencies. Catastrophes, however, occur in life, which the most abundant health and opportunism cannot overcome. Mrs. Trollope turned a blind eye on such contingencies, and carried on no matter what happened.

Being unprovided with introductory letters, this English traveller was aware that she had no special claim on American attention, nor, indeed, being sensible, cheerful, and strong, did she expect more civility than she was accustomed to at home; her troubles originated in her being accorded less. Educated in a society as ordered as the planetary system, in which everyone from squire to cowman kept his station, sudden adjustments were necessary to live in a world divested of every rag of privilege. There could be no reason for a person plunged into new circumstances of this sort to make careful observations and notes, as other indulged visitors might have to do, on this difference and on that, since in her own person she experienced the surprise and pain of trying to fit into so foreign a life. Merely to keep a record of everyday contacts was enough in her case to produce a readable and valuable book. That it was, when complete, in the main unfavourable to Americans can be no surprise once it is understood what the conditions of her life really were and what the difficulties she had to contend with. Two out of the three and a half years she lived in America were spent in Cincinnati, at that time a crude and rapidly expanding town full of bumptious pioneers. In New England, which to many English travellers appears a second homeland, she never set foot.

Some writers have asserted that Fanny Trollope's great refinement and love of luxury made Western life intolerable to her, but there is no reason to suppose, either from her books or from her upbringing, that she was finicky, self-indulgent, or even sensitive. She liked her comforts and she liked civility, but except for these weaknesses she was usually hard on herself and at times displayed a quite Spartan endurance. As Fanny Milton, daughter of an English clergyman, she had few luxuries, and as Fanny Trollope, wife of a chancery barrister, she had little scope for self-indulgence. Her story was simple. Marrying Thomas Trollope from her father's rectory at Heckfield in 1809, she set up house in Keppel Street, Bloomsbury, close to the home of her brother, a War Office clerk. There the young couple entertained their friends at five o'clock dinner round a table lit by tallow candles and were waited on by a footman in livery. For amusement they would go to the pit of Drury Lane to see Mrs. Siddons act, or drive out in their gig to picnic in the country. Five children were born in Keppel Street before May 1815, and so rapidly expanding a nursery prompted Mr. Trollope, whose wife adored open-air life, to build a house on leased ground near Harrow, lay out a garden, and hire land to farm. He named the house after the Julians estate near Royston in Hertfordshire, a property which he expected one day to inherit from his maternal uncle, Adolphus Meetkerke. The Trollopes made "Julians" their only home in 1817, but the breadwinner drove up daily in his gig to London to work in dingy chambers in Old Square, Lincoln's Inn.

It did not take Fanny many years of married life to discover that she had joined fortune with an erratic person. As a young man he had shown great promise at the Bar, was undoubtedly clever, and at one time hard-working, but as a husband turned out to be undependable both as to earning capacity and temper. He was devoted to his wife but became moody and irritable on small provocation, nagged at the children whenever they were unoccupied, and scolded so tiresomely at whist, for example, that people refused to play with him. Then again he would jeopardize their little fortune by speculating in houses and land. Giving needless offence to clients by his manners and becoming feckless in business, he by degrees lost the position which his intellect and industry had originally won for him. Suffering acutely from megrim, which heavy doses of calomel failed to cure, he had the worry of knowing that he was losing his practice at the Bar. In every way but one—lack of business capacity—his wife was a contrast to this tall, thin, moody man. She was short and plump, with a bright face and Saxon colouring.

For some years life at "Julians" went well enough. The little boys, who had been taught Latin by their father, were one by one entered as day-boarders at Harrow School in preparation for Winchester. Their mother who had tearing spirits entered into all their interests and made a very jolly home for them. They skated, botanized, bird-nested, played games, and hunted the hare in Wembley Park. Theatricals amused Fanny Trollope as much as they did the children, and scenes from Molière and Shakespeare were constantly in rehearsal. There was much going and coming of people. Herman Merivale the elder, Macready, Miss Mitford, the Miss Garnets, Lady Milman and her son Henry, Professor of Poetry at Oxford, and Miss Frances Wright are some of the recurring names.

Miss Wright, another Fanny in an age of Fannies, was an unusual person, and for a time her life came to be closely intertwined with that of Mrs. Trollope. She and her sister Camilla, both wards in chancery, were daughters of an intellectual Dundee merchant, friendly with Adam Smith. Orphaned and financially independent, the girls led lives of erratic impulse. Fanny was the more daring of the two, for at eighteen she rejected religion and marriage with a flourish and declared herself a disciple of Epicurus. Her first work—

A Few Days in Athens—gave an account of Epicurean teaching. From it she extracted a precept to "think for herself" which became the guiding principle of her life. This principle in terms of action meant do as you please, and it led her down some of the odder by-paths of experience. Her book was dedicated to Jeremy Bentham, her father's friend, to whom she later paid more direct homage.

Casting about her for a cause to employ her wits upon, she happened to read Botta's *War of Independence in the United States of America*. The narrative stirred her profoundly. A country dedicated to freedom—could anything more sublime be imagined? Calm sister Camilla listened to transports of enthusiasm and in deference to Fanny's fear lest the story prove a myth, submitted to being whisked off to see this wonderful spectacle at first-hand. Travelling to New York the Miss Wrights stayed with Mrs. Wilson, the widow of Wolfe Tone, who helped to colour their views of England, in which tyrannous old country, she opined, from the accounts of the collapse of war industries and the widespread unemployment, that a political revolution must be imminent. The sisters made friends with Mr. Charles Wilkes, cashier and later president of the Bank of New York, Dr. David Hosack of Columbia College, and Colonel John Trumbull, the artist.

Frances Wright gained considerable notoriety by her play *Altorf*, in which she had vainly tried to interest the manager of Covent Garden, Charles Kemble. It was produced at the Park Theatre, New York, with

Wallack in the title rôle. A prologue was provided by young Wolfe Tone, and a preface, lauding America, was supplied by the playwright. Failure to get the play produced by a London manager made her pessimistic as to the future of the English theatre. To her mind the dignity of English tragedy had already degenerated into pantomime, and stage tricks and fine scenery had been substituted for poetry, character, and passion. In England insurmountable obstacles stood in the way of anyone who "might ambition to correct the fashions of the stage". No such difficulties existed in America. "Here is the country where Truth may lift her voice without fear: where the words of freedom may not only be read in the closet, but heard from the stage. England pretends to an unshackled press, but there is not a stage in England from which the dramatist might breathe the sentiments of enlightened patriotism and republican liberty. In America alone might such a stage be formed; a stage that should be like that of Greece, a school of virtue; where all that is noble in sentiment, generous and heroic in action should speak to the hearts of a free people, and inspire each rising generation with all the better and nobler feelings of human nature." *Altorf* had only a moderate success at each of its three presentations in New York but was more appreciated by the sober-minded people of Philadelphia. Thomas Jefferson wrote to compliment her on its publication in book form.

The sisters returned to England in May 1820, after travelling in the north-eastern States of the Union, and Frances published—with Longman, to whom Mr. Trollope had given her an introduction—*Views of Society and Manners in America*. To her mind the overwhelming fact of American life was that the people governed themselves, and this exciting discovery caused the writer to look at everything transatlantic through rose-coloured spectacles. "My own enthusiasm", she admitted later, "conspired to throw a Claude Lorraine tint over a country which bore the name of Republic." Jeremy Bentham read the slim, panegyrical volume and promptly offered the hospitality of his house in Queen Square Place to the author. She as promptly accepted and enjoyed the society of her old and completely deaf admirer, as well as the company of some of his younger friends, George Grote, Francis Place, and John Stuart Mill.

Lafayette, who made a point of buying every book published about America, also read the little volume and wrote expressing the hope that he might make Miss Wright's acquaintance. She responded by rushing over to Paris and wept with emotion at meeting this stockily built man of sixty-three, with his large face, broad based and tapering to the forehead. His brown wig and alert manner made him appear almost too young to be greeted as the "venerable friend of human liberty". Speaking of the Americans, he said, holding both her hands, "You have only rendered justice to them; they are the best and happiest people in the world". Invited to his country house, she stayed there off and on for three years on the pretext of writing his life, to the great irritation of his family. For a time her life oscillated between La Grange and Queen Square Place. When it was Bentham's turn to enjoy her companionship in London, she would write of her doings to Lafayette: "It is now seven, the dinner hour of my Philosopher, till that time I seldom see him, but from that time I remain in his study till eleven. . . . An hour's conversation with my Socrates leaves me more fatigued than does a walk of six miles. . . . I am only half alive when away from you. . . . I love you very, very much; I put my arms round the neck of my paternal friend."

The General's daughters and sons-in-law objected more and more strongly as time went on to Miss Wright's prolonged visits to La Grange. Begging for the favour of "legal adoption" for herself and her sister, she met with obdurate resistance from his family. In vain did Frances Wright urge: "You must be our father, not in a doubtful and covert way, but in an open and manly one. We will together assume the place of children to you, we will call you father." No matter how often the old man called them "the tender daughters of his choice" no impression was made on his relations; indeed such endearments appeared to them but the onset of senility, so firmly determined were they that these rather eccentric Scotswomen should not force their way into a French family.

Drawn by Miſs L. Adams.   Engraved by W. Holl.

Mʀˢ TROLLOPE

FANNY TROLLOPE

From a portrait by Auguste Hervieu

§ II

Of all the friends who came and went at "Julians" Frances Wright was the most original and exciting. Outwardly attractive, tall and slender, with well-cut features, curly auburn hair, and blue eyes, she drew notice on herself by wearing trousers, a tunic with a sash and a broad-brimmed hat instead of a bonnet. Her emancipated views on marriage and birth control made her unlike the domesticated women of the Harrow circle, and there was no subject, however unusual, that she could not and, indeed, would not discuss.

With considerable amusement Fanny Trollope studied this modern woman. Would every girl, she wondered, be as emancipated in time? Even Thomas Trollope appeared to be diverted by her unconventional ways and seemed not only to enjoy discussions with her, but to be glad to meet the French and Italian political refugees with whom she was associating in London. She spoke much about her life in Paris, where she had an apartment, of her visits to the Chamber of Deputies, of her friends Benjamin Constant and the Comte de Ségur, and above all of General Lafayette. When it was suggested in the late summer of 1823 by his wife's old friends, the Miss Garnetts, who had migrated to Paris on the death of their father in 1820, that Mr. and Mrs. Trollope should come over to see them, he jumped at the idea and was delighted that Harriet Garnett should take rooms for them in the Rue de Grenelle.

To reach France they left Harrow in the gig at

3 A.M., drove to the Tower Stairs, embarked for
Calais at 7 A.M., and reached the French coast in
the evening. A warm welcome awaited them in Paris,
and they found themselves introduced into a delightful
world, for the Garnetts made them acquainted with
Washington Irving, Fenimore Cooper, and Mr. Wilkes.
A more agreeable dip into American society it would
be hard to bring about. The eldest Miss Garnett had
married Mr. Stone of Washington, and in this way her
sisters had come to acquire many transatlantic friends.
At the Wright salon, which gathered once a week, they
had the honour of meeting General Lafayette, who
was friendly and invited them on a ten-day visit to his
home, La Grange, in Seine-et-Marne. What between
seeing Talma and Mademoiselle Mars and all the sights
of Paris the Trollopes had a wonderful time.

On the last evening of their stay the Wrights gave
a farewell dinner in their honour. General Lafayette
was present and talked much to Mrs. Trollope of his
forthcoming tour through America. His dear daughters
Camilla and Frances had some thought of accompanying him to watch the spectacle of American gratitude
displaying itself to a foreigner who had helped them
to win independence. One of their common interests,
as Mrs. Trollope probably knew, was the manumission
of slaves. As a young man he had bought a plantation
in French Guiana, which he had with youthful fantasy
named "La Belle Gabrielle". On this estate he had
educated negroes for freedom—after all, it was a hobby
like any other, but a hobby on which George Washing-

34

ton had complimented him. Long ago, when the blood had run more swiftly in his veins, he had spoken his mind to John Adams, and had told him that, whatever the complexion of the enslaver, it did not alter the complexion of the crime which the enslaver commits— a crime much blacker than any African face. Of course the Revolution had swept "La Belle Gabrielle" away with many another colonial estate, but it was still some satisfaction to him to know that the negroes he had caused to be educated by priests of the Seminary of the Holy Ghost in Cayenne did not commit the atrocities that had taken place on other plantations.

His dear daughters, as Mrs. Trollope no doubt was aware, had the intention of buying a property in America in which to try and work out a scheme for emancipating slaves, a beautiful objective in which, had he been younger, he would have liked to participate. "Never", wrote Mrs. Trollope in her journal, "did I meet with a being so in every way perfect."

At this time Lafayette was in financial straits. He owed about one hundred thousand francs in France and since La Grange was the property of his wife he had tried to mortgage La Pointe Coupée, his marsh near New Orleans, to the Barings in London. When they refused the loan he applied to James Brown, American Minister in Paris, for an advance of money. Discredited by his attempts at military conspiracy against the Bourbons and by his connection with the Carbonari, it seemed improbable that he would be returned to the Chamber of Deputies at the elections of 1824. There was every reason for him to leave Europe for a time. Mrs. Trollope knew nothing of his difficulties, but she did know that the sisters Wright had lodged a large sum of money in America in the hope of persuading their adoptive father to settle there with them. What amusing lives some people do map out for themselves, to be sure, reflected Fanny, as she thought of her difficult life at Harrow, of the responsibilities involved in the care of five children and a sick and unsuccessful husband. For a moment she longed to shake off all trammels and travel with these attractive women. Yearning for adventure pulled her forward, affections and strong sense of duty pulled her back, but, as time was to show, the American lure was strong enough to break down all conventional resistances when the opportunity came.

The return to "Julians" put unorthodox ideas out of her head for the time being. There was so much to be done: cricketing flannels to be made for the two Winchester boys; suits to be cut down for Anthony; girls to be educated and dressed; and worst of all, financial affairs to be tackled. In May 1825 a cheerful letter and a half-crown tip were despatched to big Tom at Winchester. Money was scarce, for the Trollopes' position had altered for the worse since the uncle, whose estate they counted on inheriting, had married again and had a child. This fact depressed Mr. Trollope. He had banked so surely on having a comfortable income for his old age, and now he saw himself dependent on his own efforts and conscious of being less and less fit to exert himself.

There were many worries; neither parent really liked keeping little Anthony as a despised day-boy at Harrow, dressed in mended clothes handed on from brother to brother. Tom, the eldest son, had gone to Winchester in 1820 as a scholar, Henry had followed him in 1823, but was found to be idling there with no prospect of improvement. As it appeared to be waste of money under the circumstances to keep him at school they decided to have him taught the rudiments of business in a Paris counting-house. Some time in 1826 the three Trollopes were again staying at La Grange and hearing all about the wonderful American tour General Lafayette had made with his son George Washington and his son-in-law Le Vasseur. The hospitable Americans had sent him home on the frigate *Brandywine*, a delicate compliment, since he had in that battle come in contact with a British bullet. In spite of his family guard of son and son-in-law he was able to give her much news of Frances Wright. The sisters, it appeared, had followed the General at a day's interval round the cities of Philadelphia, Baltimore, Albany, Troy, and Boston. Later they had been with him in Washington, where he was received by President and Senate and given two hundred thousand dollars and a township of land in Florida. He then had gone on tour through the Southern States and had approved the sisters' choice of an estate near Memphis where the experiment was to be made of educating the negro for freedom. The plans for this experiment, to be known as "Nashoba Settlement", he had submitted to Chief Justice

Marshall and his old friends Madison and Monroe. Everything, he believed, was now in order, and the prospectus had been published in Baltimore in September 1825, under the title of *A Plan for the Gradual Abolition of Slavery without Danger or Loss to the Citizens of the South*. He had had a rather painful last interview with his dear Frances on the subject of adoption, but as Mrs. Trollope, being a family woman, would understand, it simply could not be done.

Unkind foreigners like Duke Bernard of Saxe-Weimar laughed at the way masculine Miss Wright "tagged" after the General and was ignored by American society. No depreciatory remarks, however, reached Fanny Trollope's ears. She was free to idealise her remarkable friend without reserve.

The year 1827 found the Trollopes anxious about a vacancy for Anthony at Winchester, and still more anxious about money to the point of vacating "Julians" for a smaller house at Harrow Weald, which they named "Julians Hill".

Their fortunes and their spirits were ebbing rapidly when Frances Wright turned up to stay with them and proposed a new project—nothing less than migration to the United States. Supposing Fanny Trollope were to come out with her to New Orleans, see her plantation, then set up in business in Cincinnati, where everyone was making a fortune,—how would that be? But the children? objected Fanny Trollope. The children! rejoined Fanny Wright, why, what a chance it was for the children! Henry could be educated for nothing on the most up-to-date socialist lines at the Robert Owen Settlement of New Harmony, while the girls could probably be taught for a while at Nashoba. It was all so easy,—Mr. Trollope could stay behind to raise capital and buy merchandise, and the other two boys could remain at Winchester till there was a home ready for them to come to on the other side. Why, before Fanny could look round they would all be making their fortunes. Queer, speculative Thomas Trollope was greatly attracted by this absurd scheme; he wished to participate in it, and, as he was so seldom attracted by anything, his eagerness encouraged his wife to fall in with Fanny Wright's proposals. Auguste Hervieu, a French artist and political refugee, who was making a prolonged stay at "Julians Hill", was also entangled by the idea, and, when Fanny Wright offered him the post of drawing-master to the Settlement, he accepted it with grateful enthusiasm. Thus it came about without any exactly designed project that Mr. and Mrs. Trollope of Harrow found themselves undertaking to found a bazaar in a pioneer community in America.

A good deal of contriving was necessary to carry out so radical a change in family life. After much discussion it was decided that Cecilia and Emily were to go with their mother, that Henry, with his knowledge of business, was to be in the first contingent, and that Mr. Trollope, possibly accompanied by Tom, would follow on later. Anthony, in any case, was to be left behind to complete his education in England.

Mr. Trollope gravely undertook to raise capital, buy

stock for the projected bazaar, and meet his wife in Cincinnati in the late spring or early summer. Meanwhile,
she and the children would spend the winter and early
spring inexpensively on Miss Wright's estate. Supposing things had gone according to plan something might
possibly have come out of the scheme, but it foundered
hopelessly, as the two main supports, Fanny Wright and
Thomas Trollope, proved completely undependable.

Somehow the money for the expedition was raised;
it is possible that Miss Wright helped them with their
passages, for it came about that, on Christmas Day 1827,
the English sailing-ship *Edward* glided with them towards the mouth of the Mississippi. On her deck stood
a comfortable, smiling figure in bonnet and shawl, whose
blue eyes beamed with kindliness, a slender woman in
a straw hat and tunic, three half-grown children, a
French gentleman in a tall hat and frock-coat, and an
English footman. Seven weeks of salt junk and ocean
views had made these London passengers long for
land. The children gazed with attention towards the
country of virgin forest and buffaloed prairie so often
described to them by their mother. Suddenly Fanny
Wright pointed down dramatically to a muddy tide,
thrusting out into the blue Mexican Sea. "The River!"
she cried, "Look, that is the father of waters!" The
young persons stared obediently over the ship's side
at the brown water; it was not much to look at after
so long a voyage, but better things were in store for
them, whirling pelicans in the sky and afar gently
emerging mud-flats and a faint line of coast. Other

signs of life gradually showed themselves—giant bul-
rushes, alligators, and the Belize pilot.

§ III

A long voyage offers many occasions for discussion
and outpouring of heart. Mrs. Trollope ended the trip
in an ecstasy of admiration for Miss Wright, who had
now come to have a halo about her head. Her statue-
like, Grecian figure, her solemn expression made her
more like a prophetess than an ordinary woman. What
a privilege it was to companion such an idealist! Who
could tire of listening to such eloquence! Who could
fail to admire the resolution she had shown in seeking
a suitable property for her noble purpose, going even
to the length of obtaining the personal advice of General
Jackson! It was a stirring story, for in response to his
suggestion that she should prospect on the newly
acquired Indian lands in Western Tennessee, Fanny
Wright, escorted by George Flower, had ridden to
Memphis and had bought a beautiful estate situated on
Nashoba River, thirteen miles below Chickasaw Bluffs,
then had ridden back to Nashville to buy slaves, while
her male companion went on to Illinois to arrange to
move Camilla Wright and his own family in the spring.
Having bought her slaves, Miss Wright superintended
the erection of huts from an inn in Memphis, and
ordered blankets, green baize, calicoes, checks, and
plaids from a firm in New York for the comfort of her
dependents. Early in the new year of 1826, when her

sister Camilla and the Flowers arrived from Illinois on a flat boat much delayed by ice, the experiment was begun.

Two other men, James Richardson—a medical student who carried out his theories of free love in a practical way at Nashoba—and Richeson Whitby, an amiable, weak Owenite from New Harmony, had been persuaded to take part in the venture. Mrs. Trollope was told that the work of clearing, fencing, and planting had been desperately hard in the beginning, but the result—an apple orchard of five acres, fifteen acres of corn, a nice potato patch, some excellent log cabins for white people and shacks for the coloured—was most satisfactory. Fanny confessed that she had begun by labouring with her black slaves, piling brush and rolling logs from dawn to dusk, but hard work had broken her down and, most regretfully, she had been obliged to leave her sister to carry on the enterprise, while she had been to Europe with one of the trustees of the Settlement—Robert Owen—to recuperate. How fortunate that journey had been in enabling her to persuade her dear Fanny to sojourn with her for a while in this paradise of Nashoba!

The economic scheme on which the experiment was founded was explained at length to Mrs. Trollope. Each slave was to earn enough money to redeem himself. For example, the initial cost of one hundred slaves would be forty-one thousand dollars. After deducting six per cent on this invested capital, there should be a net profit of ten thousand dollars per annum. The sum to be earned by each negro was six thousand dollars plus six per cent on capital outlay. After earning this sum they would have redeemed themselves and be transported outside the United States, possibly to Haiti. Discipline was to be maintained without a lash by explaining to the slaves that misconduct would mean lengthening the term of service.

Evening after evening was spent in exchanging confidences, but Fanny Trollope was woefully conscious that her stories of life in London were drab beside the perilous, stimulating narrative of her beautiful friend. Life at Nashoba would have been still more pleasant than she anticipated it would be if Leigh Hunt and Mary Shelley had also been persuaded to embark with them, as at one time it was hoped might be possible; but so far Fanny Trollope remained the only European recruit.

There was something about the way Fanny Wright talked that made every feature of American life enchanting to dwell upon. She saw the country through a golden haze and imparted her enthusiasm to her friend. It was a land where you received civility rather than service and in which that delightfully social institution, the boarding-house, enabled you to mix easily with Americans. In towns, for example, especially in new towns, all the men of business took their dinner in the principal hotel. It was an excellent way of becoming acquainted. There were no conventional barriers, there was no stand-offishness, one could speak with anyone and be sure of getting a pleasant, helpful answer. Such a picture of perfection was drawn of a country where no one was poor and everyone was obliging, that Mrs. Trollope's expectations rose high. She was prepared to like everything and everybody.

Reverence was the real sentiment inspired in her breast by her eloquent companion. Could anything be more moving than Fanny Wright's description of her dear General in Boston, laying the foundation-stone of the Bunker Hill Obelisk, that great index of freedom which was to point for all time to the sky? Could anything be more saintly than her intention "to seclude herself for life in the deepest forests of the Western world that her fortune, her time, her talents might be exclusively devoted to the cause of the suffering African"?

It was her solemn conviction, she assured Mrs. Trollope, that the negro had as good a brain as the white man and, if educated, would equal him in accomplishment. She was naturally anxious that her friend should watch, perhaps assist in the experiment, and get some first-hand knowledge of the problem to be dealt with.

The fact that Fanny Wright had already been twice to America was a great prop to Fanny Trollope, who with all her optimism must occasionally have wondered what the children would find to do at Nashoba. However, the fact that she belonged to a generation brought up on *Paul et Virginie* and on Rousseau's theories of the nobility of the savage made it natural for her to view with expectant delight the Indian, the African, and the "eternal forests of the Western World".

Immediately after taking their baggage to an hotel in New Orleans, the Trollope family started off to walk through patches of green palmettos and thread its way under close-growing trees festooned with grey Spanish moss. Feeling "rather sublime and poetical" owing to the aboriginal nature of their setting, "some of the party", presumably the children, "enjoyed commodious swings". Streaming with sweat, stung by mosquitoes, the poor young things romped round and had some fun. A crop of scarlet peppers, an orange hedge, and other exotic sights thrilled them, as did the songs of negro boatmen wafted from the river. Their mother's heart was melted with compassion by the coloured people. "I wove some little romance of misery round every man, woman, and child I met." Later on she learnt to laugh at her sentimentality.

Hervieu made a curious drawing of the bonnet shop in New Orleans, in which Mrs. Trollope was given her first lesson in equality by being formally introduced to the saleswoman, Miss Mary Carroll, who later gave up her work as milliner to run a philosophical bookshop in connection with the New Harmony experiment. In this sketch Mr. McLure of New Harmony, a benevolent figure, is seated at the counter, Miss Wright is by him dangling her straw hat and showing her ringlets, while Mrs. Trollope, dressed in poke bonnet, bertha and voluminous skirts, stands with her back to the spectator. No time was lost in discussing education with Mr. McLure, and it was soon arranged that Henry should go to school at New Harmony, Indiana, and that he should pay for his keep, as did all other pupils, by field labour.

In spite of Fanny Wright's mission, which Mary Carroll said made her name anathema, many Southern gentlemen declaring that "they would not be surprised if Miss Wright should, one of these mornings, find her throat cut", the visit to New Orleans passed off without untoward incident. After a week of pottering about in the city which Mrs. Trollope found very much like a French provincial town, the party embarked on the *Belvidere*, a paddle steamer, for Memphis, the nearest point to Miss Wright's estate. Men and manners on the *Belvidere* proved rather disillusioning: colonels and majors of militia sprawled everywhere with wads of tobacco in their cheeks and in their remorseless spitting spared nobody and nothing. The cabin carpets were soiled, the ladies' dresses ruined; there was nowhere to sit save on the edge of the bunks. At meals, too, table manners left much to be desired: food was bolted and teeth picked with knives or anything handy, and the talk raged, as it was election year, round the respective presidential merits of Jackson and Adams. "I would infinitely prefer sharing the apartment of a party of well-conditioned pigs", snapped Mrs. Trollope.

The boiler of the *Belvidere* was heated by logs, and every few hours more fuel was taken aboard from a "wooding station". The Trollope family skipped off the boat whenever this happened and looked, maybe, at a cotton-field, a sugar-cane crop, or perhaps into the faces of miserable, agued wood-cutters. Only those persons who had made a failure of everything else took on the unhealthy job of living by the bank of the river cutting and piling cords of wood. Mrs. Trollope began to observe that some people go to the wall, even in happy, egalitarian America.

When the *Belvidere* tied up at Memphis, a town perched on a bluff above the river, wide at this point as a lake, it was midnight and rod-like rain poured relentlessly down. Steamers were only warped alongside for ten minutes or so to disembark passengers before proceeding up-stream. Miss Wright hailed friends on the jetty and willing hands helped the Trollopes to scramble into a freshly made dirt road leading up to the town. Shoes and gloves were lost on their quadrupedal progress, and they reached the newly built "Grand Hotel" in a "deplorable state". The best rooms, quite bare and reeking of damp mortar, were put at their disposal; sound sleep, however, overcame them and they rose next day to the adventure of driving to Nashoba. As the sodden state of the country made all movement impossible, they were constrained to spend the day in the hotel. Fifty people came in to dine, among them the Mayor of Memphis, a friend of Miss Wright's, and many shopkeepers, who gobbled their food in silence and coughed incessantly. When they had gone, another set of diners took their place. Mrs. Trollope sat near the hotel-keeper's wife and her footman, William, sat opposite. This was another practical lesson in equality and it made her wonder a little whether her idol had not exaggerated the social pleasures of America.

In view of the delightful drive through the forest the

children were in good spirits, and, after one false start, the party set out in a "dearborn", a kind of waggonette constructed to clear the tree stumps, which stood in the path—one could not call it a road—it was a mere track cut through the forest, which "became thicker and more dreary looking every mile they advanced".

As the carriage came to a standstill at Nashoba, Mrs. Trollope's castle of dreams crashed; all the romance associated with life in the wilderness evaporated at one touch of reality. Before her eyes was a clearing some few acres in extent, around it was a zigzag fencing, and inside the fencing stood five cabins partitioned into two rooms each, and encircling all stood the silent, inhospitable jungle of Tennessee. A more deplorable-looking compound never greeted an English woman's eyes. The day was very damp and very hot, the shacks, in which Miss Wright proposed her guests should live, were severely primitive, there was no water to wash in, no sanitary convenience, no beverage of any kind except rain water. For food there was a little wheat bread, which was used sparingly, and a larger supply of Indian corn bread which the Trollopes found uneatable. There were no vegetables but rice and the few potatoes they had brought with them; no butter and no cheese. All cooking had to be done by the ladies.

As the Trollopes walked round the estate on the evening of their arrival they felt the grey, primeval forest, which stood close against the fence, to be menacing and strange. It blanketed them from the world.

So must many pioneers have felt in the old days towards the vegetation that constantly encroached about their clearings. The robust, conquering spirit of the explorer had yet to be developed in these English children, who were inclined to give way to tears and fears as they involuntarily contrasted their present predicament with their happy home at "Julians Hill".

The two Fannys shared a bedroom. "It had no ceiling and the floor consisted of planks laid loosely upon piles that raised it some feet from the earth. The rain had access through the wooden roof, and the chimney, which was of logs slightly plastered with mud, caught fire a dozen times a day." Brave Camilla, who had endured life in the wilderness for two years, looked deplorably ill, and at once confided all her symptoms and worries to the receptive ears of the newcomer. It was an awful tale, and convinced Mrs. Trollope not only of the great risk to health, but of the extreme impropriety of launching innocent children into such a community. Camilla, poor thing, had done her best in conjunction with Richeson Whitby to run the settlement on the lines laid down by her imperious sister, but how was it possible to control the slaves without the lash or the presence of Fanny? Personally she had given it up as a bad job and married Richeson, an action her sister was unlikely to approve of, but Mrs. Trollope, as a woman of the world, would understand how difficult her position had been and how lonely it was. to be there as a spinster battling with refractory blacks. "Yes," she went on in response to

Mrs. Trollope's lifted eyebrows, "even the children are refractory." Her sister's theory was that they should be educated by themselves and only allowed to see their parents in the presence of the manager, but that did not work at all; the compound was too small, you could not keep them apart. What was to be done when Lolotte's children beat Willi's children, deeming it permissible as hers were a little the fairer? It seemed useless to explain to people so rooted in inequality that in the eyes of the promoters of the settlement all colours were equal in rank. Then again, a swing had been put up for the recreation of the slaves. It had been used in "a riotous manner" and so they had decided to forbid them this amusement. Then again, the big slave Henry had declined to coulter, saying he had a pain in his knee-joint, which nobody believed, but how was Henry to be made to go coultering against his will? Nobody knew.

Camilla felt ill; both she and Richeson Whitby were on the verge of a breakdown. Tears trickled down her cheeks as she talked to the sympathetic and appalled Fanny Trollope while her masterful sister was dealing with the business of the settlement and reducing her dependents to order by moral suasion. The slaves, Camilla added, complained of having so many masters and mistresses and no one of them seemed to have any grasp of the principles that animated their owners. How academic and mad was the whole Nashoba scheme, thought Mrs. Trollope, and what fools we have been to be sucked in by empty theories of this kind. All the while Camilla talked she was wondering how best to extricate her family from the wicked situation in which her folly had landed her.

"Think of this difficulty," said Camilla, "Isabel, a slave, laid a complaint against Redrick, another slave, for coming to her bedroom during the night and endeavouring without her consent to take liberties with her person. Fanny's view of the sexual relationship", said Camilla pathetically, "has been repeatedly stated, and my husband informed the slaves that the conduct of Redrick was a gross infringement of that view." Nellie, another slave sleeping with Isabel, had gone so far against the spirit of the place as to ask for a lock for her door; it had been refused as being in its proposed use inconsistent with the doctrine of the settlement, which was that the consent of both parties was the condition of physical union, a doctrine Fanny was determined to enforce since she was sure it would give greater security to every woman than any lock could possibly do. Mrs. Trollope gave a wry, disillusioned smile and squeezed Camilla's hand. "Vividly dreadful" was her comment on everything at Nashoba.

Poor Camilla, what an awful time she had had trying to carry out these preposterous precepts, and how ill she looked, and, as for Fanny, the halo had quite gone, it was impossible to believe from dress, look, or manner she could be the same person whom in Harrow and Paris she had admired and, on the boat, had come to idolise. Intensely and unaffectedly surprised to see that her guests did not find Nashoban ways to their liking,

Fanny Wright walked apart as if in lonely ecstasy and made her meals off a bit of corn bread and a cup of rain water, smiling as she did so with the complacency of a saint in the wilderness. It was immensely aggravating to her English guest to see how sublimely contented she appeared to be. Was she mad, or had she no sensibilities? Such idealism was perilously near fanaticism. How could she ever for one moment have thought of persuading friends from Europe to come and spend months in this horrible, desolate, unhealthy place? There was simply no explanation save that their hostess lived in an imaginary world.

If Fanny Trollope was shocked, Hervieu was horrified. "Where is the school?" he asked of his hostess. "It is not yet built" was the answer. Enraged, he wept and determined to return to Memphis at once. Before driving away he made the dismal and faithful sketch of the settlement which illustrates Mrs. Trollope's book. As they parted she assured him that she would join him with as little delay as possible.

By the 26th of January the Trollope family were back in Memphis. It was just a month since they had landed and already all plans for living cheaply were frustrated. Auguste Hervieu determined to throw in his fortune with that of his English friends, and, while waiting for an up-stream steamboat, they discussed Nashoba and their own immediate plans. There was nothing for either of them to do in Memphis, and it was not a healthy place. They were advised that Cincinnati was in every way superior. There seemed nothing for it but to go and wait in this "Queen of Western Cities" till Mr. Trollope and his consignment of goods turned up.

On the 30th of January Camilla and Richeson Whitby left Nashoba to recuperate in the North. Fanny remained alone in the settlement until relieved by the Whitbys in June. Her devotion to her cause was admirable but profitless, since by June she had made up her mind to abandon the settlement and make arrangements for the transportation of her slaves to Haiti.

§ IV

With outward composure and cheerfulness the Trollope party set off in the *Criterion* for Ohio. Whatever happened the children must be encouraged to think all was for the best. At Louisville, on the south or Kentucky shore of the river, they landed and poked round the town and its vicinity; the country was so pretty that Mrs. Trollope would like to have stayed there, but it was said to be a fever district "during the warm season" and therefore not to be considered as an abode for the family.

On the 10th of February they reached Cincinnati, a finely situated, featureless city, "without domes, spires or steeples", with about twenty thousand citizens, which included a colony of three thousand free negroes known as "Little Africa". The travellers made their way to the Washington Hotel, and found some sixty or seventy men were feeding at the table d'hôte; Mrs.

Trollope and her party joined a smaller table, at which the women of the establishment were eating. The rooms of the hotel gave an impression of gloom, for all windows were darkened by suspended rolls of wallpaper, which did duty as shades or blinds, rather awkwardly, as they had to be rolled up and fastened with strings to the window-frames, whenever light or air were wished for. These wallpaper shades were to be found at that time in every part of America and were possibly responsible for the curious, universal habit to-day of keeping blinds half drawn at all times of the year and in all weathers.

Nothing that savoured of privilege was tolerated at the Washington Hotel. Mrs. Trollope, innocent of the feeling of the country, ordered tea in her room for the children and herself. An obliging Irishwoman brought it. Presently sharp knocking was heard at the door: it was the portly landlord. "Are any of you ill?" he asked. "No, thank you, sir, we are all quite well", replied Mrs. Trollope. "Then, Madam, I must tell you that I cannot accommodate you on these terms; we have no family tea-drinkings here, and you must live either with me and my wife, or not at all in my house." An excuse that they were strangers and did not know the customs of the country did not placate the democratic ire of the landlord. "Our manners are very good manners," he retorted, "and we don't wish any changes from England." Abandoning the argument, Mrs. Trollope silently resolved to move into a house of her own the next day. This feat she accomplished with the assistance of Auguste Hervieu and her servant William. It was not a convenient residence that she had lighted on, for it had no drain, pump, or cistern, and there was no visible means of getting rid of garbage. Sending for the landlord she asked him how it should be disposed of. "Your help", he replied, "will just have to fix them all into the middle of the street, but you must mind, old woman, that it is the middle. I expect you don't know as we have got a law what forbids throwing such things at the sides of streets; they must just all be cast right into the middle and the pigs soon takes them off." The activity of the pigs reconciled her to having her skirt nuzzled as she walked down Main Street by "snouts fresh dripping from the kennel".

Getting a "help" was a constant difficulty. Girls condescended to come and work for a week or two and then walked off. It was taken as an insult to ask for a reference for character, and the word "servant" could not be mentioned. Mrs. Trollope, who was nothing if not good-natured, adapted herself as best she could to the rôle of friend rather than mistress, made clothes for the "helps" so that they should not spoil their own frocks, and treated them kindly. One girl agreed to come provided her "mother's slave" could be allowed to cross the river from Kentucky and assist her once a week with the cleaning. When Mrs. Trollope refused at the end of two months to lend her money enough to buy a silk dress to go to a ball, she left saying: "Then 'tis not worth my while to stay any longer." Another girl turned up saying, "I'm come to help you", and told credulous Mrs. Trollope that as she had "got religion" she would like to be spared to go to Meeting every Tuesday and Thursday evening. Mrs. Trollope conceded this, and Nancy proved an excellent maid and always had an open Bible near her when working. One day she fell sick of the cholera. During the two nights Mrs. Trollope sat up with her, all her delirious thoughts rambled heavenwards. "I have been a sinner, but am safe in the Lord Jesus", she repeated. On recovering she borrowed three dollars and went for change of air. While she was away a neighbour called in to inform Mrs. Trollope that Nancy was a most abandoned female. There was nothing for it but to tell the girl on her return what she had heard and to terminate the engagement. The girl, to Mrs. Trollope's surprise, took it quietly, bade everyone a civil good-bye, and left without making a scene. Soon after this episode a satisfactory household was made up by engaging "a worthy Frenchwoman" and "a tidy English girl" to do the harder work of the establishment.

The marketing Mrs. Trollope and Monsieur Hervieu found to be very amusing and very cheap. There is an illustration in *Domestic Manners of the Americans* which probably is a portrait of the artist himself returning with a basket of vegetables on his left arm and a ham in his right hand. Fanny often rose at four in the morning to chaffer and bargain with the country people over their wares, and her joviality of disposition went down well. Beef and mutton were twopence a pound, a chicken could be had for sixpence and a turkey for two shillings. Fish from the river were cheap and fruit was plentiful, though in no way to be compared with the slowly ripened produce of English gardens. Yellow peaches, gritty strawberries, and water melons, however, were eaten by the children with great enjoyment. Tomatoes were about sixpence a peck and all other vegetables moderate in price.

The companionship of Auguste Hervieu was an immense comfort to Fanny Trollope. To have someone in a wilderness of strangers with whom she could discuss plans and talk of home just made life tolerable to her, but it caused neighbours to talk. Who was this Englishwoman who had left her husband to settle in an American city? Where was Mr. Trollope? Who was Monsieur Hervieu? The social leaders of Cincinnati held aloof from such a curious household and waited to see what would happen. It was said that these queer people were about to hire a building for some odd purpose. Some said it was to be a theatre, others a concert hall or dancing-room, and others something worse. The general sentiment towards foreigners and their ways was hostile, and Mrs. Trollope's every action was watched by many suspicious eyes.

With attentive curiosity did she and Auguste Hervieu examine the shops and amusements of Cincinnati. They found two well-patronized museums, housing waxwork figures, which at that time were a novelty. Monsieur

Dorfeuille, of Louisiana, owned the Western Museum, which contained natural history specimens and a chamber of "Horrors", in which were displayed bloody knives, hatchets used by murderers, ropes that had strangled criminals, and wax figures in the very act of taking life. The supreme attraction of the dreadful room was "The Head of Hoover", the actual head of a murderer in a huge glass of alcohol, all swollen and distorted. Dorfeuille's manager was young Hiram Powers, later to win fame as a sculptor, but at that time inventing accordeons and talking dolls. Hervieu made friends with his compatriot, and Mrs. Trollope took a fancy to Hiram. They put their heads together and evolved between them a "Pandaemonium" such as Mrs. Trollope had seen in Europe. She and Auguste designed the scenery and suggested the tableaux, while Hiram Powers made the figures. A scene from Dante's *Inferno*—a *bolgia* in fact—was the notion. Dwarfs and giants, ebony imps, whose eyes darted out flames, and monstrous reptiles devouring youth and beauty, all were there. Iron bars charged with electricity separated spectators from this "hell", but its success was great and the pressure such as to cause many shocks provocative of giggles and dismay. Mrs. Trollope wrote a verse of invitation to "Hell":

> Come hither, come hither by night or by day
> There's plenty to look at and little to pay;
> You may stroll through the rooms, and at every turn
> There's something to please you and something to learn.

If weary and heated, rest here at your ease,
There's a fountain to cool you and music to please;
And further a secret I still have to tell
You may ramble upstairs and, on earth, be in Hell.

Other verses followed prophesying an awful doom to
any mortal daring to approach its bars. She also drew up
a catalogue for Dorfeuille with four folio pages of translation from the *Inferno*. In fact the Western Museum
became a sort of playground for the Trollope family.
At one time Henry was acting the part of "The Dis-
appearing Lady" in a magical entertainment there.
Doctor Timothy Flint often looked in after visiting
his son's book-store on Main Street to enjoy the latest
novelty devised by his English acquaintances.

A few people were sufficiently interested in the fine
arts to encourage Monsieur Hervieu to begin work on
"a noble, historical picture" of the landing of General
Lafayette at Cincinnati. Like his friend Sir Thomas
Lawrence, Hervieu preferred to paint portraits, but
orders were hard to come by, so he compensated
himself and flattered his friends by portraying them as
spectators in an historic scene.

Among the rare places of amusement in Cincinnati
was a rose garden, in which people ate ice-creams on
holidays, ice-creams being then a new luxury. When
first opened, a signboard was put up showing a Swiss
peasant girl holding a scroll begging guests not to
gather the roses. Her red skirt revealed ankles; ladies
shuddered and intimated to the proprietor that, if he
desired their patronage, he must lengthen the skirts,

and thereupon a flounce of blue was added to the red.

Indoor amusements were few, as billiards and cards were forbidden by law. Indeed a penalty of fifty dollars attached to selling a deck of playing cards in the State of Ohio. There were no public balls except at Christmas time, no concerts and no dinner parties. Evening meetings in church and chapel appeared to Mrs. Trollope to be the only social occasions at which everyone wore their best clothes. On the whole she found the Americans "a cold and dreary people", for, though endowed with clear heads and active intellects, they had no real enthusiasm, fire, or depth. "I never saw a people so devoid of gaiety", observes this joke-cracking, jovial woman. On the 4th of July only did they appear to her to unbend and become at all amiable.

The theatre at Cincinnati was small, but English Mr. Drake, the manager, and his wife were both excellent actors and gave good Shakespearean performances to poor houses, and farces and melodramas to good houses. Much as the Trollopes loved the theatre, the ways of the audience sometimes made it a dearly bought pleasure. Men sat in their shirt sleeves and threw their legs over balconies and boxes, chewed and spat and drank whisky and made the most nauseating noises. Quite a friendship sprang up between Mr. and Mrs. Drake and the Trollopes, and members of the family often walked in from Mohawk to assist at their productions.

In June 1828 bills announcing that "Miss Wright of Nashoba" was to lecture were posted at the Court House. Mrs. Trollope squeezed into the crowded building with Mrs. Price, the doctor's wife, to hear a speech on true knowledge as opposed to revealed religion. Fanny Wright held, as Fanny Trollope knew well enough, revealed religion to be one of the greatest evils afflicting mankind, but once again she was swept off her feet by "the eloquence of this extraordinary orator", and the beauty of the muslin-clad figure, which again reminded her vividly of a draped Grecian statue, once more overwhelmed her. For three consecutive Sundays Miss Wright lectured to spellbound audiences on the equal education of the sexes, on the desirability of raising women's status by protecting their legal identity in marriage and by limiting their families. The lectures were such a success that she repeated them in August at the Opera House. It was with a feeling of relief that Mrs. Trollope learnt that the Nashoba settlement was to be closed down as soon as arrangements could be made for the transfer of the slaves.

"Co-operation has nearly killed us all," said Frances with a sigh. Camilla never recovered her health after all she had gone through in the grim forest clearing, and died untimely, to her sister's lasting grief.

§ v

The payment of ordinary day-to-day expenses became difficult after the first weeks in Cincinnati, since expected drafts had not arrived from England. Auguste Hervieu, however, nobly threw himself into the breach and supported the whole party till remittances came to hand. At first he became instructor in a school of drawing, but the pupils were so undisciplined and incorrigible that he resigned. "Can you not enforce order?" he asked of his German chief. "American boys and gals vill not bear it, dey vill do just vat dey please," was the reply.

Mr. Trollope was either so dazed over his financial undertakings or so wrapped up in his new occupation of compiling an "Encyclopaedia Ecclesiastica" that he omitted to write to his wife for weeks after her departure. Mrs. Trollope had resided in Cincinnati four months when she despatched her ninth letter to her husband. By the same packet she wrote to Tom: "I cannot express to you the dreadful anxiety to which this silence gives birth. Is your father ill? Is he dead? Have his affairs fallen into such confusion that he has not been able to procure the money necessary to send us a remittance? Wherever you may be, my dearest Tom, when you receive this, I entreat you to write to me immediately. Our situation here would be dreadful were it not for Monsieur Hervieu's grateful, generous kindness. It is more than a month since we have had a mouthful of food that he has not paid for. How are you, my darling boys?"

Attracted by the idea of getting Henry educated for nothing, Mrs. Trollope had sent him to New Harmony. She had received a good account of the settlement from the Wrights, but unfortunately by the time Henry reached Indiana, McLure had gone to Mexico, leaving his French mistress in charge. Under her direction the education paid for by the manual labour of the pupils had been abandoned and replaced by more digging, sowing, and reaping. Henry soon fell ill and after two months was brought back to Cincinnati, where under doctor's orders he was half killed with calomel and bleeding. It was May when he reached his mother; the weather was uncomfortably warm, the garbage smelt unbearably, and mosquitoes shrilled all day and all night. For the sake of the emaciated boy, it became urgent that they should move to the country. With some difficulty Daniel Gano was persuaded to let them his house, Gano Lodge, by Howard's Woods in the village of Mohawk. It was but a mile and a half from the city, but the relief of moving out of streets was immense and Henry began to recover at once. The peaceful little frame house faced the forest. It was painted white, had green shutters and a deep piazza, which overlooked a field with a potato patch in one corner. There was a plank track from the entrance gate to the house, which was shaded by great locust trees. Enough grass to graze a cow and a rough kind of lawn where they could have tea pleased everybody. In high spirits Mrs. Trollope led her family out walking. At first they pushed their way joyously through the forest and "crunched knee-deep in aboriginal leaves", but this pleasure soon palled; the forests became objects of detestation, they were stuffy below, tangled above, treacherous of foothold and full of rotten branches, water-holes, stumps of old trees, snakes and other crawling things. As Mrs. Trollope says with that snap which is characteristic of herself, "they were grim and stove-like". The absence of flowers and shrubs made excursioning monotonous. To people accustomed to the oak woods of England with their clean undergrowth of hazel and blackthorn set with patches of bluebells and primroses, these dark, steamy, flowerless forests were hateful. However, the summer passed happily enough between boating on the Ohio and excursions in the Kentucky pastures. As flower hunts were out of the question, fossils were sought for instead, since the children had discovered the soil to be crammed with millepores. Studies were carried on in the piazza, books were read, journals kept, and then there were always bazaar plans to discuss.

Henry's illness had brought them into contact with a kind physician, Doctor Price, whose wife amused Mrs. Trollope while his girls acted with her children. "La!" said Mrs. Price one day when she and Mrs. Trollope were discussing religion, "the doctor don't think anything more of the Bible than of an old newspaper . . . but then doctors have their opinions." Even strong Mrs. Trollope had to consult Doctor Price, for the heat did not suit her; she became very thin and found the vicissitudes of temperature "most extraordinary". Though she believed in walking as a means of keeping well, Cincinnati was a pork-pickling centre at this time and the killing of pigs in any spot adjacent to any brook made many country walks disagreeable. Thousands of beasts were driven in from the oak forests to be slaughtered beside the river port. Great expertness was shown in the dismembering of the animals, but it did not make for amenity that they could be dispatched anywhere, and, as Mrs. Trollope observed, any lady's slipper might light on pigs' tails and jaw bones and be withdrawn all stained with blood on almost any rural path. To climb the sugar-loaf hill in the vicinity of their Mohawk home, the Trollope family had to cross an odiously red stream.

For some unexplained reason Mr. Trollope delayed sailing from England, but remittances began to reach his wife in June, which enabled her to furnish the Lodge more comfortably, and by the time her husband and Tom appeared on the scene in early September, quite a cheerful family party greeted them. Once again Mrs. Trollope began to entertain. Jose Tosso, leader of the local orchestra, relates that he played one evening at a party given by her to about a hundred young people. A French play—*Les Deux Amis*—was acted, in which Mrs. Trollope, Henry, Doctor Price, and others took part. Tosso remarked on the excellence of Mrs. Trollope's French. *The Merry Wives of Windsor* was also acted by the young Prices and the young Trollopes. Henry played the part of Falstaff with a pillow stuffed under his waistcoat. He had imbibed a good deal of sack—some people thought him drunk—but he played the part in so rollicking a manner as to make everybody rock with laughter. After the plays there came supper and then dancing till daylight. Tom looked back in his old age on very happy days in Cincinnati.

Mrs. Trollope thought fit to write cheerful letters to friends at home. It would be foolish and humiliating to confess to failure, more especially since "many short-sighted mortals had deemed her in the worst stage of lunacy when she left the Old World to pay a visit to the New". "Write to me", she begs Miss Mitford, "in this remote but very pretty place where I am sitting to hatch golden eggs for my son Henry. . . . The country is beautiful and wonderful in its rapid progress towards the wealth and the wisdom, the finery and the folly of the Old World; and I like it well—the better certainly that while Henry is making money I am saving it." Her rather pathetic struggle to keep up the appearance of success is all the more remarkable when one knows the real truth. Before Mr. Trollope left Cincinnati she wrote: "Henry's prospects here are, I think, very good: but eighteen is too young to be left, too young to be judged of fixedly. I believe him to be very steady, but I must watch by him for a year or two longer. I think Mr. Trollope returns to us next year and I shall then be able to decide whether it will be advisable to continue here or not." In order to create a good impression she allowed herself considerable latitude of statement. The girls, for example, were alleged to be studying under very good masters and in no way to be wasting their time. "Nothing shall keep me here", she writes, "after my eldest girl is sixteen—at least, nothing that I can possibly foresee or imagine, as I think I owe it to her to let her see young ladies' daylight in a civilized country."

§ VI

Mr. Trollope, of course, had not worked according to schedule, since he had arrived without any of the requisites for the projected bazaar. He planned to stay with his family till after Christmas and then to return to Europe and order fancy goods for despatch to Cincinnati. It was disappointing to Fanny that he had not carried out the agreement arrived at at "Julians Hill" ten months previously, for his failure to do so meant that no stock-in-trade could possibly reach her before June of the following year. Some people had no sense of the value of time: it was a natural deficiency and the best had to be made out of it, as of other bad jobs. It was, however, obvious that the idea she had cherished of hiring some building to serve an immediate purpose had now lost its point; perhaps it might be better to occupy her enforced leisure with devising something rather more elaborate than she had originally thought of. Instead of adhering to the scheme of a bazaar pure and simple, it might be possible to work the selling of fancy goods into some more comprehensive scheme, in which amusement and business should go hand-in-hand. Cincinnati was deficient in so many things. When one came to think of it, there was nowhere to eat icecreams when the rose garden was under snow; little exclusive suppers could not be given in the local hotels;

there was no coffee-house; the public dancing-rooms of the place were even less cheerful than the cold Assembly Rooms of provincial towns in England. Numbers of good reasons sprang up in Fanny Trollope's mind for letting her fancy run riot in new plans. By degrees she came to convince herself and her family that a ballroom, supper apartments with retiring-rooms for ladies, duly supplied with mirrors and toilet tables, a panorama of London, a mart in which amateurs could expose their works for sale, and a museum of objects of European interest should be tacked on to the bazaar. The more the Trollopes let their imagination roam, the more convinced they became that it would be better to build than to adapt any existing structure to their now magnificent purpose. Together with Hervieu they set out to design something as unlike as possible to the grim utilitarian streets being ruled rectangularly in all directions around them. The monotony must be broken and some note of romance and witchery introduced to stimulate these cold automata known as Americans to flights of fancy towards Bagdad, Luxor, or even Xanadu. With evident memories of the Pavilion at Brighton in their minds, they drew the plans for a fantastic, amusing building. Something between an elegant Regency green-house and a Turkish mosque was the result.

Unfortunately Mrs. Trollope is completely silent about this enterprise in her book. Possibly she did not consider it relevant to her thesis, possibly also she did not wish people in England to know that she had tried to set up in trade. Whatever the reason for her mumness, there is no allusion to the bazaar in *Domestic Manners of the Americans* save the cryptic hint that some "speculation" was proving unsuccessful.

Just as Mr. Trollope and Tom had decided to return to England they heard that President Jackson was about to visit Pittsburgh and was landing at Cincinnati on his way. They at once made up their minds to travel by the same boat, and on hearing of his arrival at Louisville laid their plans accordingly. A large crowd gathered on the bank to greet the new President and, "great enthusiasm being neither the virtue nor the vice of America", it gave a very faint cheer. Carriages awaited the presidential party, but General Jackson was a simple person and preferred to walk. He took his tall hat off to the people, revealing thick grey hair "carelessly arranged". "In spite of harsh, gaunt features he looks like a gentleman and a soldier," commented Mrs. Trollope in her diary. "He was in deep mourning, having very recently lost his wife." Amid the silence she heard two remarks: "There goes Jackson! Where is his wife?" and "Adams forever!" Mr. Trollope and his son walked up to the hotel, took the opportunity of being presented to the President, and then secured berths on board the steamer by which he was travelling.

Writing of the trip to his wife, Mr. Trollope expressed himself as deeply disgusted by the brutal familiarity to which they saw the General exposed in every place at which they stopped. There was not a husky lad from a keel boat who was not introduced to the President unless indeed they introduced themselves in this way: "General Jackson, I guess". The General bowed assent. "Why, they told me you was dead." "No, Providence has hitherto preserved my life". "And is your wife alive too?" The General, apparently much hurt, signified the contrary, upon which the man said, "Aye, I thought it was one or the other of ye."

On his way through New York, Tom went to call on Fanny Wright. He found her sitting at an office table with William Owen, surrounded by manuscripts and proof-sheets. Since leaving Nashoba she had become editor of the New Harmony *Gazette* and had bought the old Ebenezer Church near the Bowery in which to lecture. She had renamed it the Hall of Science. Mrs. Trollope, on reading copies of the *Gazette* some months later, found it very dull and said no one from Bossuet to Cunningham could produce more yawns from a given number of pages.

Mrs. Trollope was much drawn towards Mr. Bullock, proprietor of the Egyptian Hall of Mystery in Piccadilly, who owned an estate two miles down river on the Kentucky shore. Both he and his wife became intimate with Mr. and Mrs. Trollope, and it is possible to trace the effect of this intimacy on the rear façade of the bazaar, which obviously was designed in emulation of the London Hall. The Bullocks' own house was greatly admired by Fanny as really "civilised", and the gems of art it contained showed "as strangely in this wilderness as would a bed of roses in Siberia". Both husband and wife appeared almost as much out of their element in Ohio as she was. They were "wasted" there, but still their companionship was delightful to her and such a contrast to that of most of her acquaintance with whom nothing worthy of the word conversation could be had. Except for the well-known Doctor Timothy Flint, ex-minister of the Gospel and editor of the *Western Monthly Review*, she found no one worth talking to in Cincinnati. He, however, was extremely friendly, often invited Mrs. Trollope to his house, and presented her with his novel, *Francis Berriam*. Hervieu paid him the same compliment he had already paid to Dorfeuille and Hiram Powers of painting him into his picture of the landing of Lafayette, though he was not present on the occasion of the General's visit. Doctor Flint found his way into Mrs. Trollope's good graces by deprecating the American habit of "puffery", a trait peculiarly obnoxious to this English traveller.

Doctor Timothy Flint, in spite of his frontier life as a missionary on the Mississippi, found Mrs. Trollope "singularly unladylike" and "badly dressed". That she was a voluble talker and fond of mimicking people did not tend to make her popular. The social handicap she had imposed on herself by arriving in a strange town accompanied by a Frenchman who was not her husband naturally caused a lot of "tea-table talk". Doctor Flint was convinced she was perfectly "moral", but in spite of his recommendations no one in Cincinnati would receive her. He got tired of telling people she was "amusing", "endowed", and "a blue-stocking dyed-in-the-wool". No one would invite her to their houses save "four respectable families" who never gave parties. How could this short dumpling of a woman, "a mere war of frock and petticoat", an "inelegant female" in short, hope to enter the fashionable houses of Cincinnati without so much as one credential or letter of introduction? She was so set in her own opinions that he never could persuade her that the new stores of the city provided all the fancy goods she was preparing to sell. "Incapable as an infant" of running any business concern in her own country, how could she hope for anything but ruin in America?

One evening Mrs. Trollope met a scholar and discussed poetry with him. They spoke of Pope. "Oh!" said the scholar, "he is entirely gone by in our country. It is considered quite fustian to speak of him." She protested that *The Rape of the Lock* showed some talent. He shook his head and exclaimed, "The very title!" Shakespeare, she pleaded. "Shakespeare, madam, is obscene, and thank God we are sufficiently advanced to have found it out." Chaucer and Spencer he dismissed with a word, as they wrote in a language which no one now understands. What can one expect, however, she reflected, in a country devoted to the reading of newspapers? As far as she could observe, no one ever read any other kind of print. The newspaper had already begun to expel the book from the life of the people. The many outlooks presented by books which compel to selection and criticism, were being replaced by the authoritative voice killing the need for individual expression of opinion and making the buying of books a mere luxury. Every little town, in Mrs. Trollope's day, was producing its *Clarion* or *Sentinel* or *News*, and most people were not leisured or educated enough to feel the want of anything else. Every American newspaper, owing to shortage of current news, showed a tendency to become a magazine, and furnished stanzas by Mrs. Hemans, garbled extracts from Moore's *Life of Byron* or a few short sentences comparing Bulwer's novels with those of Scott. It was difficult for Mrs. Trollope to think that things would ever be different in a country in which whisky was but tenpence a gallon and tobacco grew like a weed. The twin vices of drinking and chewing alone must suffice to keep the men at a permanently low level.

Class consciousness was carried so far that everyone seemed anxious to show himself better than Mrs. Trollope. Her country neighbours were all so scared of being patronised that they could not say "thank you" when offered small kindnesses or civilities. Sometimes people condescendingly told her that they were beginning to understand her "broken English". It was always difficult, they said, to understand people from London, for London slang was the most dreadful in the world, and people who lived there always put an *h* where it is not and never put it where it is. They could easily see that Mrs. Trollope was taking pains to learn the American way of pronouncing, since she did not misplace her aspirates. One woman asked her gravely if she had left home "in order to get rid of the vermin with which the English of all ranks were afflicted." A man remarked to her with an affected yawn, "I wonder you are not sick of kings, chancellors, archbishops and all your fustian of wigs and counts. I protest the very sound of it sends me to sleep."

She often thought of Fanny Wright when she heard women alluded to as "females" or "the fair sex". How scornful she would be to know of the strange prudery of Cincinnati, where it was impossible to have a picnic party as it was considered "indelicate" for ladies to sit down on the grass with gentlemen. Shirts could not be mentioned in mixed company, and a young German saying "corset" bolted, blushing, when he saw the effect of his words. At the George Washington Birthday ball Mrs. Trollope found the gentlemen had a splendid supper set in a large room, while the excluded females dallied with candies in the corridors. And as for the ballroom it was a deplorable spectacle: the women sat in rows round the walls and waited until some beau was good enough to give them a turn. It was against the rules for a girl to leave the room with her partner, so the moment the turn was over she was replaced in her row to await another invitation. Even in boarding-houses men and women sorted themselves out and sat apart at different ends of the table.

Some of Mrs. Trollope's conversational experiences are almost unbelievable. A casual acquaintance approached her one day by saying, "Don't you hate chintzes, Mrs. Trollope?" "No, indeed, I think them very pretty," was the answer. "There, now," exclaimed the questioner, "if that is not being English! I reckon you call that loving your country. Well, thank God, we Americans have got something better to love our country for than that comes to: we are not obliged to say we like nasty filthy chintzes to show that we are good patriots."

"Chintzes?" said Mrs. Trollope, greatly puzzled, "but what are chintzes?"

"Possible! Do you pretend you don't know what chintzes are? Why, the nasty little stinking blood-suckers that all the beds in London are full of."

It is obvious from this and other recorded talks that Mrs. Trollope's associates were not of the educated families of Cincinnati. "The better people", as we know, fought shy of her, considering it very odd that any "well-balanced woman" should remain any-where except "in the custody of her husband". If only General Lafayette had written to her earlier she would not have had to submit to this tiresome ostracism, but it was not till fifteen months after her arrival in Cin-cinnati, and then only in response to an urgent appeal, that a kind letter reached her from the General, sym-pathising over her Nashoban experience. "I wondered at the determination of a London lady to make herself a forest pioneer. . . . I admired the effect of *her* elo-quence, the warmth of *your* friendship. . . . I grieved to hear you had left Nashoba after a visit of eight days. No explanation was obtained from Fanny, who only in a kind word mentioned your departure." The

General enclosed notes of introduction to Mrs. N——
and other residents in Cincinnati requesting them to
make Mrs. Trollope's stay among them agreeable.
"I am very much pleased with these letters of Lafayette", writes Mrs. Trollope; "they contain the first
certain assurance that we are not a set of accomplished
swindlers."

§ VII

In spite of what Mrs. Trollope says of the lack of
culture in Cincinnati, literary coteries and debating and
musical societies did exist and flourish—we know it
from other sources. Indeed there was a society there
which, according to Mr. James Handasyde Perkins,
could hardly be equalled in any city for intelligence.
It consisted of an East End set of "fashionables" and a
West End set of "intellectuals". The Footes, leaders
in the West End set, were living in the town when
Mrs. Trollope arrived, and the Semi-Colon Literary
Club, of which Harriet Beecher was a member, met
once a fortnight at the houses of Mr. Foote, Mr. Greene,
and Mr. Stetson, and was the last word in culture.
Mrs. Trollope knew neither East nor West End set
and never was invited or noticed by the Semi-Colon
clique. She never met the Beecher family, Doctor Drake
or many other well-known people who would have
made life pleasant for her. The fact that she knew but
few people in Cincinnati and met no one of importance
in Washington or New York was well appreciated by
Harriet Martineau. When asked at a dinner at Mr.

76

Hallam's house what Mrs. Trollope's position in the
United States had been, she had "no scruple in saying
Mrs. Trollope had no opportunity of knowing what
good society was in America", and that she had
thought proper "to libel and slander a whole nation".
Her hearers were silent and she thought they acquiesced in her judgement, but Mr. Milman put in a word
for his old friend Fanny Trollope. Had she not as a
matter of fact been ill-used, taken in, perhaps, over her
bazaar? "No doubt," said Harriet Martineau, "any
English traveller who begins the game of diamond cut
diamond with Yankee speculators is likely to get the
worst of it." There could be no doubt she was abun-
dantly cheated, hence this form of vengeance, a vitu-
perative book. Mr. Milman quietly observed he knew
by his acquaintance with her what hard usage she had
to complain of. "Oh, yes," said jocular Mr. Rogers,
another of the guests, "Milman is acquainted with
Mrs. Trollope; he had the forming of her mind." This
raised a hearty laugh and Mr. Milman reddened. The
talk passed to other subjects, but next day Harriet
Martineau received a call from Mr. Milman. He said he
had not educated Mrs. Trollope, as he was about the
same age as she was, and added, "Unless you feel bound
in conscience to expose her—which might be to ruin
her—I would intercede for her". Laying his finger on
the proof-sheets of Harriet Martineau's own book on
America, he said: "Can't you now say what you think
of these same people and let that be her answer?"
Nettled, Harriet retorted, "Why, you don't suppose

I'm going to occupy any of my book with Mrs. Trollope. I would not dirty my pages with her stories, even to refute them. What have I to do with Mrs. Trollope but to say what I know when inquired of?"

After all, Miss Martineau had been wafted through America on billows of approbation. She had gone there as a personage; what could she know of the seamy side of American life, and how could she be expected to sympathize with such a sordid record of failure?

In English provincial towns it was always possible, at the time Mrs. Trollope lived, to find a pleasant educated clerical circle. Except for Catholic bishop Fenwick and Doctor Timothy Flint, this type of society was completely lacking in Cincinnati. Religion was in the hands of any tinker or tailor who could set up a conventicle, and the display of individual whims in matters religious was most irritating and distasteful to one brought up in the Church of England. Revival meetings in chapels were bad enough, but there was something about a camp meeting even more shocking to an Anglican, religious exercises and emotions of a year, sometimes of a lifetime, being crammed into one stifling week of conversion. Mrs. Trollope attended one of these gatherings on the edge of the backwoods of Indiana with Mr. and Mrs. Bullock. They drove to the ground cleared for the meeting. A circle of tents, and behind them another circle of vehicles and tethered horses, were illuminated by a bright moon and numerous bonfires. The lights among the trees, the crowds, reminded Fanny of Vauxhall, but at the corners of the enclosure were "four high frames constructed in the form of altars". "On one of these were supported layers of earth and sod on which burned immense fires of blazing pinewood. On one side a wide platform was erected to accommodate the preachers, fifteen of whom attended this meeting and, with very short intervals for necessary refreshment and private devotion, preached in rotation day and night from Tuesday to Saturday."

When Mrs. Trollope arrived the preachers were silent, but . . . from nearly every tent came sounds of praying, preaching, singing and lamentation. She was inclined to enjoy the picturesque scene and then thought to listen at a tent flap. What she heard we do not know, but it "furnished realities that could neither be mistaken nor forgotten". Someone raised "the drapery" from a tent so as to allow the interior to be seen. "The floor was covered with straw, heaped in masses at the sides, and a close-packed circle of men and women kneeled on the floor. A figure in black stood praying and preaching—the auditors called on Jesus with groans and sobs." Mrs. Trollope looked into many tents, one of them full of negroes: each had for her the aspect of Bedlam.

"At midnight a horn sounded through the camp which we were told was to call people from private to public worship; and we presently saw them flocking from all sides to the front of the preachers' stand. . . . There were about two thousand assembled. The preaching began, sinners were adjured to come forward to 'the pen', hymns were sung." For a moment Mrs. Trollope felt the beautiful effect of this woodland worship and watched the many fair young faces lit by moonbeams, then she was plunged once more in horror and disgust, for penitents had come forward and were going through convulsions of repentance in "the pen". The preachers moved among them. "I heard the muttered 'Sister! dear sister!' I saw the insidious lips approach the cheeks of unhappy girls; I heard the murmured confessions of the poor victims, and I watched their tormentors breathing into their ears consolations that tinged the pale faces with red. . . . At length the atrocious wickedness of this horrible scene increased to a degree of grossness that drove us from our station." A rueful figure withdrew to her carriage to rest at 3 A.M. and rose two hours later to find the congregation enjoying a camp breakfast.

Harriet Martineau was particularly vexed with Mrs. Trollope's description of the camp meeting. In some degree she felt it was an attack on Nonconformity and therefore protested angrily against it: "She knows nothing but the Established Church, everything else appeared queer and wrong to her . . . she is a mere cockney as far as religion is concerned. Her unceasing employment is to find out blemishes in forms of worship. How could the fathers and husbands and brothers of America", she asks, "permit the revival scenes described by Mrs. Trollope—those mystic caresses, those scenes that made Mrs. Trollope shudder?" How surprised Miss Martineau would be to find that American writers to-day regard Fanny Trollope's descriptions as in the main accurate and well observed, which is not to say that they agree with any moral deductions drawn by the writer from the scenes described.

Religious dissipation was always popular in pioneer society, and when, in the second week of May 1829, Robert Owen, who had challenged the whole religious public of the United States to discuss with him publicly the truth or falsehood of all the religions ever preached, appeared in Cincinnati to meet the Reverend Alexander Campbell, of Bethany, Kentucky, who had taken up the gauntlet, he had an attentive audience. The Methodist Church put at the disposal of the disputants held a thousand persons, and Doctor Flint was in the chair. Half the seats were reserved for men and half for women; the building was packed. Owen was a charming speaker, and though like Fanny Wright he denounced Christianity as a fraud, the feeling left upon his hearers was that they were in the presence of a man of great benevolence who loved the whole human family. Mr. Campbell rose and quizzed Mr. Owen unmercifully on his doctrine of human perfectibility and made the audience rock with laughter. When he sat down Mr. Owen jumped up and enunciated his "twelve fundamental laws of human nature". Then Mr. Campbell spoke again, but each speaker merely made a statement of his own case and in no wise answered the arguments of his opponent. Though no debate in the strict sense of the word had taken place, the speeches had been found by many auditors to be a pleasant entertainment.

The spring and summer of 1829 passed quickly. Mrs. Trollope walked in from Gano Lodge every morning to superintend the building of the pavilion. So long as money was forthcoming to pay costs and wages, the bazaar was regarded as an embellishment to the city. It was an exotic novelty, and though its situation —on Third Street, a little east of Broadway—was some quarter of a mile away from the haunts of fashion, many people strolled along on Sundays to see how "the old English woman's building" was getting on. We may read in a local directory for 1829 of its "rapid progress towards completion" and a description of its plan. The basement, which was entered by three flights of steps from the street, contained a coffee-house, bar-room, exchange, and parlour for commercial business. Overhead was a "compartment" sixty by twenty-eight feet, through which "passed" two rows of columns. Stalls for the display of "chains", "guards", "stationery", "useful and useless articles of dress", and "pellucid porcelain" stood here. In the rear was "an elegant saloon opening into an Exhibition Gallery", where Hervieu's "superb picture" of the landing of Lafayette was hung. Above this bazaar there was a "magnificent ballroom" with an orchestral gallery. Three large arabesque windows received the rays of the sun or emitted "the rival splendours of gas-illumined walls". At the back of the ballroom were private cabinets that could be hired for the select supper parties of the *beau-monde*. A "Rotundo" on the top of the building was designed for the exhibition of pictures. The arabesque windows made a pleasing impression from the street, as did the light double stairway leading to the first floor. The façade at the back was dignified with Egyptian columns in the style of temples by the Nile. The front of the building measured eighty feet in width and eighty feet in height, its depth was one hundred and four feet. It will be understood from this description how very carefully the Trollopes had planned this pavilion. It was designed to attract to itself all the artistic and social activities of the town, as well as to serve as the meeting-place for men wishing to transact affairs. Mr. Palmer, the architect, and Mr. Delany, the installer of the gas illumination, worked with enthusiasm in carrying out the original ideas of these queer English people who were incapable of checking accounts or criticizing contracts. Mrs. Trollope doled out some thousands of dollars on account, but when the final bill was presented it amounted to twenty-four thousand dollars, about twice as much as she had reckoned on having to pay. It was very disconcerting, but with her usual buoyancy she told the contractor that all would be well in the end if only the bazaar could be opened. So they continued, but terror overtook Auguste Hervieu and the children late in August 1829, for Mrs. Trollope fell desperately ill and seemed likely to die. For nine weeks she lay in bed, being bled and dosed with calomel by half-teaspoonfuls. When her robust constitution had thrown off the illness, she had to give in to extreme lassitude caused by the treatment, and spend all her time reading. At first Mr. Flint's Mexican novel *Francis Berriam* beguiled her convalescence, then she read *Hope Leslie* and *Redwood* by Miss Sedgwick, then all Mr. Cooper's novels, then, finding she could not sit upright, much less stand, she deserted American fiction to read *Waverley*, and worked her way through all Sir Walter Scott's romances. By the time she had finished this course she was less weak, and it was Henry's turn to be ill again. Valiant-hearted and feeble, his mother rose from her sofa to nurse him. Frank and kind as always, she was able to cheer up the family and laugh for the children's sake, though she knew the earth was trembling beneath her feet.

For a few days during her illness goods had been sold and Hervieu's picture exhibited in the bazaar, then came the apprehension by the builder that no more than twelve or thirteen thousand dollars would ever be paid to him, so the building and its contents were impounded, which meant that some ten thousand dollars' worth of the crated French and English fancy goods, which were awaiting Mrs. Trollope's convalescence to be unpacked, were also forfeited. Soon after getting home Mr. Trollope wrote that he had bought and despatched goods to the value of two thousand pounds to his wife. These had reached Cincinnati safely, and now they were exposed for sale by the contractor for anything they would fetch. The department stores of the city picked up bargains, for sold in this way nothing realised so much as its cost. Dismayed but undaunted, Mrs. Trollope immediately began to think out other expedients for financing her family. The idea of a book of travels had been forming itself in her mind. If only she could write as well, let us say, as her friend Miss Mitford, what pictures she might draw of the people in Cincinnati—"so very queer, so very unlike, any other thing in heaven above or earth below". "I amuse myself by taking notes and hope some day to manufacture them into a volume. I think that if Hervieu could find time to furnish sketches of scenery and groups, a very taking little volume might be produced." By degrees she came to pin all her hopes of financial salvation on the completion of this work.

Pressure of creditors other than the contractors became acute, servants' wages and rent fell in arrears, such furniture as she had bought for Gano Lodge was seized. They even had to leave their home, and she and the two girls were reduced to sleeping on one small bed "at Major L——'s", while Henry and Hervieu lay on the kitchen floor. Even for this graceless accommodation she had to "trade her parlour carpet". All the time letters were coming from her husband, asking what she was doing with the two thousand pounds' worth of goods shipped, why she was not staying on in Cincinnati, and why she was trying to send Henry home. She had kept him informed of day-to-day happenings, but now it seemed useless to explain to him the catastrophic nature of her experiences. "Is it not strange", she wrote to Tom, "that your father does not yet know that these goods never brought one penny into my hands? . . . Everything from the time you left us went wrong, spite of exertions—very hard labour—on our part, that would pain you to hear of." Can one be surprised that Mrs. Trollope had no kindly feeling for the people of a place in which she had suffered so much?

There was nothing to be done at the last but to plan an ignominious exit. On this note of bankruptcy the business enterprise ended. The gaudily coloured fabric remained standing, but its promoters fled away.

The subsequent fate of the bazaar varied with the years. In 1830 gay dances were held there, at which Jose Tosso and his band played quadrilles and the fashionables of Cincinnati refreshed themselves with oysters, sherbet, and ices. The ballroom was used by day as an academy of music and dancing. A few years later the building was sold to the Ohio Mechanics' Institute for ten thousand dollars.

A British officer, Major Thomas Hamilton, who stayed in Cincinnati three years after Mrs. Trollope left, thought the building "a brilliant and fantastic outrage on all acknowledged principles of taste". At the same time he considered that it beautified the city, and said that the inhabitants had reason to be grateful to Mrs. Trollope for giving Cincinnati a "celebrity". "Ears polite", he said, had never heard of the place when she went there, but since her sojourn within its area "a zone of light has encircled" the town. At the time of his visit the bazaar was occupied by a caretaker, who

showed him over the various apartments and explained
their purpose. The lower saloon was used on Fourth of
July celebrations, but the caretaker thought it would
probably be converted into a church. Its gaudy colours
had already been overlaid with whitewash. Harriet
Martineau attended a concert in the building shortly
after Major Hamilton's visit. The bazaar appeared to
her as "the great deformity to the city". Happily it
was not very conspicuous, "being squatted down
among houses nearly as lofty as the summit of its
dome. It is built of brick, has Gothic windows, Grecian
pillars and a Turkish dome. It was originally orna-
mented with Egyptian devices, which have, however,
all disappeared under the brush of a white-washer."
As she sat in the large, plain room she reflected sen-
tentiously on the site which so recently had been a
cane brake "echoing with bellows and growls of wild
beasts". "Now the spirit of Mozart was swaying and
inspiring a silent crowd, as if they were assembled in
the chapel at Salzburg."

Captain Marryat, who was in Cincinnati ten years
after the Trollopes had left, was told by some women
who remembered seeing Mrs. Trollope walking from
her cottage at Mohawk to superintend the building of
the bazaar that it was known to the townspeople as
"Trollope's Folly".

§ VIII

When they saw the fate of the bazaar was sealed,
Auguste and Fanny put their heads together and de-

cided how best to extricate themselves from Cincinnati, make the most of their small resources and, if possible, increase them. They agreed that a book about America might have a great sale in England and that illustrations made on the spot would strengthen its appeal. It was obvious that if it dealt with Cincinnati alone it would not sell as well as if it included descriptions of places like Philadelphia, Baltimore, Washington, and New York, therefore these cities would have to be visited and described.

In all the wide American continent, Mrs. Trollope knew of but one person who might assist her in carrying out this plan, a girlhood friend, Mrs. Stone, who lived either in or near Washington. If only Mrs. Stone could be found she would certainly take the whole party in and do anything in her power to help them, and by living with her it was just possible enough money could be saved to tour America. Financial help might be extracted from Hervieu's great historical picture of Lafayette landing at Cincinnati; it could be rolled up to accompany them on their wanderings and be exhibited wherever they stayed. One never knew, it might help to pay their way. Then there were the children to consider. Henry should certainly be sent home to England without delay, for the American climate did not suit him. In spite of his high spirits, he had never really recovered from his severe illness. The girls must share in Mrs. Trollope's fate, whatever it was to be.

After discussing every aspect of the situation in the most careful way, Fanny Trollope and Auguste Hervieu decided to leave Cincinnati for Washington as soon as they could after Christmas. The first two months of 1830 were bitterly cold and ice precluded the navigation of the Ohio till the first days of March. Then the party set out for Wheeling by river, a two and a half days' trip, to catch the mail for Baltimore. None of the family had travelled by road before, and they regarded the high-hung, stepless vehicle known as a "stage" with curiosity. Mrs. Trollope describes clambering up a ladder to reach her seat, which was five feet from the ground. The roads were rutted, soft, and full of holes, the worst places were corduroyed, but whatever the substance passed over the effect was one of continual bumping, sometimes on the head, sometimes on elbows or knees. It took everybody all their time to keep their place, but the young people were in high spirits at leaving Cincinnati and nothing was vile except the ways of their fellow-travellers. Strangers addressed Mrs. Trollope as "Old Woman!" and pushed past her without ceremony into inns and houses. However irritating democratic manners might be, some compensation was to be derived from looking out on the country as they drove along. Miles of loveliness greeted their eyes along the deserted Alleghany mountain roads and glimpses of bright rhododendrons and azaleas already beginning to bud in sheltered places made up for many social solecisms, and when at last they dismounted at Baltimore they found still further pleasure in a city of civilized appearance in which the houses had pediments, where there was an excellent inn, an important cathedral, historic monuments and marble fountains. Several ships lay in the docks, among them a trader, the *Dalhousie Castle*, sailing for England. Henry was put on board with a minute sum of money in his pocket and told to make his way home as quickly as he could on landing at Liverpool. A very forlorn figure, without sixpence to his name, turned up at Harrow Weald on the 19th of April, having walked from London. Neither Henry nor Emily ever got over their dreadful experiences in America, and a few years later both were dead.

A happy fortnight was spent investigating Baltimore before embarking on a small steamer for Washington. Hervieu drew everything he could find to draw and Mrs. Trollope described everything she could see, for she had made up her mind that her experiences at Cincinnati would form half her book and that the rest must be padded out with sightseeing of the conventional sort. As the steamboat from Baltimore passed by Mount Vernon, Mrs. Trollope strained her eyes to see the cypresses waving over Washington's grave. It was difficult to find anything much to say about this beautiful river reach overlooked by the stately piazza except that it formed a suitable setting for the last years of a great man. Gadsby's Hotel in Pennsylvania Avenue housed them for their first night in Washington. It was a fashionable caravanserai, at which guests were accommodated at one dollar and twenty-five cents a day. The wooden stairways and the late hours kept by some of its patrons made it a noisy place to sleep in, so Fanny Trollope rose at dawn and shepherded her party to the Capitol. With truly English condescension she observed that she had never expected to see so imposing a structure in America; it was worthy of the older country whence its design was derived.

As they walked along they discussed ways and means and looked out for a cheap boarding-house. They were lucky enough to fall in with a quiet family on F Street, who for moderate terms accepted them for a month as paying guests. Congressional debates were assiduously attended. That members wore their hats and spat to an extent decency forbade her to describe, disgusted her, as did the Senate Chamber, which contained persons who looked like gentlemen and yet could be seen spitting with the same persistence as Congressmen. At the theatre, too, most elegant young men were observed to take wads of tobacco from the pockets of their silk waistcoats and stuff them in their cheeks and throw their legs over balustrades and sides of boxes no less freely than in Cincinnati.

While writing of the ways of the rulers of the country Mrs. Trollope went to see what the fortnightly presidential receptions were really like. With a sniff she declared that the company was "about as select as an Easter Day ball at the Mansion House". The negligent attire of the guests was certainly an innovation. Under preceding administrations men had dressed for the White House in knee breeches, silk stockings, and handsome coats and waistcoats. General Jackson, who had never been to Europe, wore trousers, black coat and stove pipe hat. Many of his friends dressed in the same way, and it was quite as much of a shock for old Washingtonians as for Mrs. Trollope to see fustian suits from Alabama and Tennessee mingling with the gold lace and court breeches of the diplomats.

"God grant", wrote Mrs. Smith, wife of the President of the Bank of Washington, "that the people do not put down all rule and rulers." Neither Mrs Smith nor her friends took to the new folks at the White House, and she showed her disapproval in quite an original way. She and her husband happened to worship in the same church as General Jackson. "The President and his family sit in the pew behind us, and I often have the pleasure of pinching his fingers, as he has a habit of leaning his hand on the side of the pew and I have the habit of leaning back. The first two or three times of his coming to church he bowed and I curtsied after church, but now we never look at each other. Neither Mr. Smith nor I have called but once at the White House. . . . Never before was the Palace so accessible. They live on equal and familiar terms and accept all sorts of invitations."

When working hours were over, Mrs. Trollope took the girls to inhale the breezes at Meridian Hill or to pick wild flowers in the grounds of "Kalorama", or Beautiful View, an estate a mile outside the city. Sometimes they ferried across to Arlington in the afternoon and wandered on the Virginia shore. As always, their pleasures were of the simplest kind.

After several inquiries Mrs. Trollope discovered that her old friend Mrs. Stone was living near the Great Falls of the Potomac in Maryland. It was a delightful reunion, for Fanny found in her the faithful friend of girlhood. Writing home she says, "The only thing that has not disappointed me is the friendship of Mrs. Stone. Nothing can exceed her kindness and with her we have found a home, the tranquillity of which has done much towards the recovery of my health, both of mind and body. But you must expect, my dear Tom, if Heaven indeed permits my safe return, to see a very old lady. My eyes have greatly failed me since my illness; I can do nothing without spectacles and I can no longer walk as I did, but I am infinitely better than when I came here and still young enough to enjoy a long, long talk with you as in days of yore."

Mrs. Stone had a large family with which the Trollope girls thankfully merged and a roomy house in which to accommodate the rest of the party. Unfortunately her income was small and she had to ask Mrs. Trollope to contribute towards the housekeeping. Gallant Monsieur Hervieu at once guaranteed whatever was required and then set out to give drawing lessons and to paint portraits. It was early in May 1830 that the family settled down in this haven of Stonnington. Many hours were spent sketching and picnicking beside the Great Falls, hunting for flowers and watching for butterflies and humming-birds. Moonlit evenings in the piazza listening to the rondos of Mozart ended the most perfect days Mrs. Trollope had spent in America.

"I am with the oldest friend I have in the world," she wrote to her dear son Tom. "She is a most agreeable woman and seems as well pleased to resume our old friendship as I am. With her I hope to remain until something can be arranged for our future plans. I fear that our means, crippled as they have been by our loss at Cincinnati, will not allow us to live decently in England until some return from the property there can help us to do so."

Writing from Stonnington in July 1830, she once more attempts to make out to Miss Mitford that all is as she would like it to be. "I have nothing to detain me now but the waiting to know Mr. Trollope's final decision as to the necessity of his once more crossing the Atlantic to arrange himself the final settlement of our untoward speculation at Cincinnati and my wish to see a few more of the wonders of this wonderful country."

She discussed many problems with Mrs. Stone and always came back to the great anomaly, slavery. Surely it was the negation of everything America stood for. And yet the slaves themselves did not look unhappy; there were plenty of smiling faces. It was not till she had been in and out of many houses and had talked with all sorts and conditions of men that she began to realise something of the degradation involved both to slaves and slave-owners. The attitude adopted towards coloured people was difficult for her to understand: they were treated in some ways as she would treat a pet and in others were completely ignored. For example, a girl who was too refined to sit down on the grass with a gentleman at a picnic would lace her corsets with a negro in the room. A Virginian gentleman told her that he and his wife always had a coloured girl sleeping on a mat in their bedroom to fetch water for them in the night or anything else they might need. Slave-owners assured Mrs. Trollope that it was impossible to teach a negro to be honest and that everything had to be kept under lock and key. The mistress of every house was followed about by a negro child carrying a basket of keys. Does it not annoy you, asked a stranger, to have this child dragging about after you? Oh dear no, came the reply, I don't notice her at all.

At one time Mrs. Trollope was in a house in Virginia when a slave child of eight found a biscuit temptingly buttered on the shelf of a cupboard. She had eaten most of it before anyone noticed what she was doing. As it was sprinkled with arsenic for the destruction of rats, Mrs. Trollope was consulted as to what should be done when it was discovered the child had swallowed poison. A large cup of mustard and water was prepared by her orders and poured down the little creature's throat. Presently she shivered so violently that Mrs. Trollope took her up on her knee. There was a general laugh among the white members of the household, and one of the girls exclaimed, "Oh my! if Mrs. Trollope has not taken her in her lap and wiped her nasty mouth! I would not have touched her mouth for two hundred dollars!"

And yet in spite of all she saw and all she heard

95

about slavery there remained no manner of doubt in her mind that it was pleasanter to live among slaves than among freemen, a sad conclusion which personal suffering had gradually compelled her to adopt. In a didactic sentence she attempts to justify her preference: "I conceive slavery to be essentially wrong, but so far as my observation has extended I think its influence is far less injurious to the manners and morals of the people than the fallacious ideas of equality which are so fondly cherished by the working classes of the white population in America." Principles or no principles, it is evident that life was more comfortable in a slave state.

During the summer a fortnight was spent in Philadelphia. Monsieur Hervieu's picture was taken for exhibition there, but it did not pay its expenses. This was a disappointment, as brilliant prophecies had been made by their friends of its success. "It may prevent our seeing Niagara," wrote Fanny. "I regret this, as I fear my book will seem very imperfect without it."

It was in Philadelphia that Mrs. Trollope bought a copy of Captain Hall's "very strange work" on America which "has put the Union in a blaze from end to end. . . ." "This hubbub made me very desirous of seeing his book, but I am glad to say that I did not succeed till after my first volume was finished and most of the notes for the second collected. I thus escaped influence of any kind from the perusal." The publisher, Mr. Lee, gave her to understand that "the agreeable captain" was under writing orders as he ever was or hopes to be again under sailing orders. "He would have done quite well enough service to the cause he intends to support if he had painted things exactly as they are without seeking to give his own eternal orange-tawny colour to every object. His blunders are such as clearly to prove he never, or very rarely, listened to the answers he received—for we must not suppose he knew one thing and printed another."

Good use was made by Mrs. Trollope of the opportunity of describing the Quaker city, and drawing attention to such peculiarities as the fastening of chains across the roads on Sundays to prevent ungodly traffic. Once again they heard Fanny Wright lecture. Beautiful as ever in her friends' eyes, she appeared on the stage of the Arch Street Theatre escorted by a bodyguard of Quaker ladies, and delivered her lecture, which by now had become stereotyped. She was listened to quietly until she stated on the authority of Jefferson that Washington was not a Christian; this occasioned a protest from the audience, otherwise the meeting was dull. An irascible Scotsman heard her speak at Philadelphia on "The Rise and Progress of Liberty in America", a subject of which he could plainly see this "venomous vixen knew as little" as he did "of the administrative details of the two-penny post-offices in Pekin". He was annoyed to hear her "utter sundry blasphemies against the Federalists, Colonel Hamilton and Mr. Jay, whom she accused of being corrupters of the mind of Washington and betrayers of their country for English gold". The fact that she could pick up "more money by talking than half-a-dozen industrious tailoresses" was also a grievance to this conservative gentleman.

By this time Fanny's slaves had been dumped in Haiti. She had chartered the brig *John Quincy Adams* of Boston and, together with William Phiqueval of New Harmony, had conveyed them to that island. This action inspired the ballad makers of the day, and a song was sung in New York to celebrate the voyage:

> Oh, Fanny Wright—sweet Fanny Wright!
> We ne'er shall see her more;
> She's gone to take another freight
> To Haiti's happy shore.
> She used to speak so parrot-like,
> With gesture small and staid,
> So pretty in her vehemence—
> Alas! departed maid.
> Tho' we are men of age mature
> How can we rule ourselves?
> Unless we all wear petticoats
> We're laid upon the shelves.

Fanny's most conspicuous days were over, since she had made the common error of falling in love with her partner on the brig, and had denied her convictions by engaging herself to marry him as soon as they could travel to Paris.

§ IX

During the early autumn Mrs. Trollope fell ill of the same low fever from which she had suffered at Cincinnati. By Mrs. Stone's advice she repaired to

Alexandria and took rooms there for the winter. The weather was severe, and carts crossed from Maryland to Virginia on the ice. The clothes they had brought from England were almost worn out and proved an insufficient protection from cold. To Tom she wrote: "Your dear sisters have had a pretty sharp lesson in economy. They mend and mend and mend. They are indeed treasures to me, and their devoted affection outweighs all my misfortunes. I often comfort myself with thinking that they would not have loved me so tenderly had they not seen me suffer. Poor Cecilia is literally without shoes, and I mean to sell one or two small articles to-morrow to procure some for her and for Emily. I sit and write, write, write—so old shoes last me a long time. As to other articles, we should as soon think of buying diamonds!

"I wish with all my soul that you could see and hear poor Hervieu. He seems only to live in the hope of helping us. He has several good pupils and has just had a fifty dollar portrait ordered. He pays our board here and set his heart on getting us home without drawing on your father's diminished purse. Sometimes my heart sinks when I think of our present dependence. But Hope tells me it is just possible my book may succeed. It will have great advantages from Hervieu's drawings. If it *should* succeed, a second book would bring money."

To a friend she wrote: "Henry's miserable health, my own narrow escape from death, the failure of our hopes of placing him advantageously and my peculiar disappointment in not benefiting him, as I had hoped to do, by this expedition, all tend (together with back-woods disagreeabilities) to make one dislike Western America. . . . America is a glorious country for Americans, but a very so-so one for Europeans."

The days went monotonously by; she spent them transcribing her notes and seasoning them with reflections of an aggressively moral character, such as "This free-born race care little for the vulgar virtue called probity. . . . Their moral sense is in every way blunter than with us. . . . The want of interest in everything that is not their immediate concern has a most paralysing effect upon conversation. . . . American women are the handsomest in the world and the least attractive. . . . Other nations have been called thin-skinned, but the citizens of the Union have apparently no skins at all. They wince if a breeze blows over them unless it be tempered with adulation." She was told by an Englishman that he had never heard Americans conversing without the word dollar being pronounced between them. This gave opportunity for some hard snapping on her part, "Such unity of purpose, such sympathy of feeling can, I believe, be found nowhere except perhaps in an ants' nest. The result is exactly what might be anticipated. This sordid object for ever before their eyes must inevitably produce a sordid tone of mind. It produces a seared and blunted conscience on all questions of probity." Hard, bitter, unfair sayings abound in her book and account for the storm of resentment created by its appearance.

In the spring of 1831, by dint of most rigorous

economy, sufficient funds had been accumulated to enable the whole party to travel. They went by way of Baltimore, Philadelphia, and the Delaware to Trenton. On the way up the Delaware River they passed the home of Joseph Bonaparte, situated on the New Jersey shore. "How strange", said a Quaker to Mrs. Trollope, "that dethroned kings should find their best home in a Republic!" Even casual remarks were grist to the author's mill. Nothing could be neglected that gave colour to the narrative.

The relief of getting to New York, saying good-bye to "I-am-as-good-as-you" manners, was extreme. It seemed to put them all in touch with Europe again. It was nice to find that Miss Mitford's play, *Rienzi*, was being performed and even that Fanny Wright was lecturing in "a Queen Mary ruff and a spencer" in her Hall of Science. All Mrs. Trollope's old interests began to revive and her galling memories of Cincinnati to fade.

She took up her pen and wrote to Miss Mitford, begging for an introduction to her publisher, Whittaker Treacher. "My book is gossiping and without pretension, most faithfully true to the evidence of my senses, and written without a shadow of feeling for or against the things described. I have about thirty outline sketches by Hervieu, not of scenery but of manners, which I think will help the book greatly. I have had an opportunity of seeing *Rienzi*: it is a noble tragedy and not even the bad acting of the Chatham Theatre could spoil it."

A lightning trip by way of West Point, Albany, and Utica to Niagara completed her American itinerary. The visit to Niagara was looked upon as indispensable to the completion of her book. To us it seems of little consequence whether she went there or not, but all the people of her generation attached an undue importance to waterfalls and would put themselves to any expense and discomfort to visit one. It seems to have accompanied a romantic love of ruins. Mrs. Trollope would have approved of the Mississippi, had it been incidented with mediaeval abbeys and fortresses.

After delivering her manuscript to Whittaker Treacher she felt rather nervous at finding out that Captain Hall was his "reader". However, her anxiety was relieved a few days later on learning that Captain Hall had reported very favourably on her book and that it was to go to press at once. *Domestic Manners of the Americans* appeared on the 19th of March 1832. A few days later "The Sacred Den " at Harrow Weald, in which she wrote, was invaded by Milman's crying "More book! more book!" Southey, Wordsworth, and Miss Mitford were delighted with the work. The press acclaimed it; Fanny Trollope suddenly found herself a celebrity inundated by invitations. Hervieu rose to the occasion by painting her portrait for exhibition at the Royal Academy.

Home life had become far more peaceable since Mr. Trollope had immersed himself in his Encyclopaedia and had withdrawn himself from legal work. "I cannot express my delight", writes Fanny, "at his having found an occupation. . . . He is quite another being and so am I in consequence."

There was a time when a good review in the *Quarterly* would have puffed Fanny Trollope up with pride; now she took faint heed of such compliments and thought only of the pence her writings would bring in. "If I can get a little money, I do not mind abuse. . . . What a Jew I grow, my whole thoughts run morning, noon and night on the possibility of getting something by this, that, or the other."

She was a little disappointed at receiving but £250 for the first edition of 1250 copies and £200 for the second edition of 1000 copies. What she expected to get one does not know. Later on further money was paid over to her which made her takings on this book amount to about £900 in all.

Anxious to get a footing in the periodical press she inquired of a friend: "What does one do to get into business with the mags. and annuals? Does one say, as at playing écarté, I propose, or must one wait to be asked? Remember dear, that I have five children!"

Side by side with the stream of success flowed a murky rivulet tending towards bankruptcy. In vain did Fanny try to stem its tide by publishing a novel, *The Refugee*, and by working madly on another novel, *The Abbess*, as well as by writing a humorous poem, *The Mother's Manual—A Guide to Match Makers*. In vain did she rush through Belgium and Western Germany in order to write a guide book for John Murray.

Creditors became importunate, and as Mr. Trollope shrank from any inquiry into their financial situation, Mrs. Trollope investigated their position with her brother, the War Office clerk. The more they found out the more hopeless appeared their predicament. Her marriage settlement, for example, had never been registered or signed by either trustee. The title-deeds of their house in Keppel Street and of other property had been deposited with various persons as security for money raised, but no receipts had been exacted, and no one knew to whom they had been made over. It was obvious that the Trollope fortunes were irreparable and that they were heading for a crash. How could it be minimised? that was the problem. A family con-clave was called and immediate expatriation to Bruges was decided to be necessary, for these were the days of imprisonment for debt. Mr. Trollope must be got out of the country at once, or the long arm of the law would snatch him from their midst. On the 18th of April 1834 Anthony was deputed to drive his father to the coast and put him safely on the Ostend packet. Five hours later bailiffs seized their house and possessions at the suit of Lord Northwick. Henry, who was ill, was sent to stay with an old friend of his mother, Fanny Brent, at Dawlish; Cecilia and Anthony were packed off to join their father at Ostend, while Fanny Trollope and Tom remained behind with their kind neighbour, Colonel Grant, to save what could be saved from the wreck of their home.

By July all the family, save Tom, were settled at the

Château d'Hondt, just outside one of the town gates of Bruges, but ill-fortune dogged them still. Henry, who was a great big fellow of eighteen, had a terrible cough and seemed very weak; little Emily showed signs of great delicacy. Doctors diagnosed consumption, and Mrs. Trollope sent Cecilia away to be with her uncle in England, in order that she might be out of the way of so much illness. If these poor children were doomed, she would have them die comfortably, well housed and well fed, and that meant settling down to ever more unremitting work. She was encouraged by a visit from John Murray, junior, in August. He showed her an excellent review in the *Quarterly* of her book on Belgium and Western Germany, and spoke cheerfully of its running into a second edition. October found her sitting up night after night toiling at *Tremerdyn Cliff*. In November Henry got rapidly worse and required continuous nursing. His mother says, "I write, though I hardly know how I can do it." Henry could not bear her out of his sight, and, with hands half-crippled by the rheumatism in her shoulders, she moved her secretaire into his room in the evening of each day, and kept herself awake alternate nights by drinking black coffee. The day before Christmas Eve Henry died, and Mrs. Trollope at once sent for Cecilia to come to Bruges and look after Emily. The family now had literally nothing on which to live but her books. She could not afford to lay down her pen for a day. It had to be driven across the paper no matter what her mood. Even though her boy lay dead there was no time to mourn; the lives of six people depended upon her being able to write steadily under all circumstances.

Fortunately, Mr. John Murray was generous with advances. She had contracted to write a book for him to be called *Paris and the Parisians*, and her husband and the two girls accompanied her to Paris to make notes for it. Then they all went back to Bruges to enable her to complete the volume and write another novel—this time concerned with life on the Mississippi—*Jonathan Jefferson Whitelaw*. Meanwhile Mr. Trollope's health gave her cause for deep and continuous anxiety. The pains in his head became worse and worse, until they drove him to live almost entirely in bed. In October 1835 he died, after having at least had the satisfaction of seeing one volume of his Encyclopaedia published by John Murray. He was buried close to the grave of their son Henry, who had been dead but nine months. After her husband's funeral Mrs. Trollope returned to England and devoted herself to the care of little Emily, but it was too late to save the child and she too died four months later. Mrs. Trollope laboured on, for there were still two children entirely dependent on her exertions.

The book that has earned for her so much abuse is, in some ways, an unsatisfying production, for it does not represent her complete life in America or reveal the reason that took her there. *Domestic Manners of the Americans* is the vehicle of a thesis: interests and incidents, which in the opinion of the author do not subserve her purpose, are rigidly ex-

cluded from its pages. For example, there is no mention
of the bazaar; the children are rarely alluded to; there
is very little about Nashoba, and literally nothing about
financial difficulties or about Auguste Hervieu. If one
knew no more about Mrs. Trollope than is revealed
in her book, one would close it with the idea that she
was an eccentric English woman who, for no adequate
reason, dragged her children out to America and
selected Cincinnati as a place in which to reside while
she settled her son in some vague business there.
Later, for no apparent reason, her husband and another
son join her, but, instead of travelling away with them
when they returned to England, she lived for a second
year in "hateful Cincinnati", and then dawdled out still
another year in Washington and other cities. As told
by her the narrative has little point, but then the point
was not in the story but in the moral drawn from it.
It is only by piecing together what other people
observed and discovered about the Trollopes that we
can arrive at any life-like picture of the strange experiences of this English family in America.

Mrs. Trollope was over fifty when her first work
appeared. Primarily intended as a warning to the
people of England and secondarily as a guide-book to
America, its great appeal consisted in her confession
of failure to adapt herself to democratic life. One conviction at least she had beaten out of her experience in
the United States: it was that "universal degradation
invariably follows the wild scheme of placing all the
power of the State in the hands of the populace". Her

conversion to monarchical views resulted in a narrative as lively and coloured as any cautionary tale. What she set down was a selection of experiences, and they were the outcome of honest purpose. She eliminated much, but it is improbable that she invented any story or statement. Males did keep their hats on in her parlour, females did enter her house uninvited, rough women did call her "honey" and slipped their arms through hers, men did chew tobacco, drink whisky and throw their legs about. No one among the pioneers read books or conversed or troubled about politeness or culture; they were far too busy—in their own phrase —in "getting along".

With all its bitterness and injustice, her book is nearer American life than other works of the time, written by authors who never mingled on even terms with the American people or were exposed to the full blast of equality in day-to-day experience. The majority of the people Mrs. Trollope came in contact with never entertained her or put themselves out for her. She was just an ordinary, unconsidered person, adjusting herself painfully to the framework of an uncouth pioneer society.

London read her book eagerly. It had a special interest for those political circles in which Reform was being canvassed. In far-away American cities, at street corners and in shop windows, placards were displayed advertising the book. It was bought as eagerly as a newspaper. Travellers coming back from the United States reported that the one question on steamboat,

stage, or in hotel was, "Have you read Mrs. Trollope?"
The more the work was abused the larger became
its sale. The author, however, derived no benefit from
this transatlantic circulation, as it was unprotected by
copyright. It is doubtful whether she cared to know
that thousands of Americans were reading her book.
Anxiety, sorrow, and hard toil were driving memories
of America from her mind. Nashoba and Cincinnati
had become as insubstantial as a dream.

FANNY KEMBLE

FANNY KEMBLE

§ 1

"THE Kembles", observed Miss Thackeray, "seem somehow a race apart." Handsome, passionate, objective, confident persons who shouldered their course through life, they had a way of making more sensitive people appear dim and devitalized. Roger, the first of the acting Kembles, claimed to come of an old Catholic family and prized Father Kemble, the martyr, as a kinsman. At thirty some vagrant instinct prompted him to join Ward's company of strollers: later he married the manager's daughter, and in his turn developed into manager. Mr. and Mrs. Roger Kemble became the parents of twelve children, most of whom turned to the theatre for their living. Though separated by eighteen years, John the eldest and Charles the youngest boy were sent to be educated at Sedgeley Park, a seminary for priests, and later spent several years at the Benedictine College at Douai. Their father hoped that one of them might hark back to the old Kemble tradition of piety, but acting was more immediately in their bones, and to the stage they went.

Their mother, a resolute woman, always ready to take any part in any stock drama at a moment's notice, acted 'Prospero' the night before Sarah's birth, and 'Ann Boleyn' the night before Stephen's. Her children, whose features suggest Jewish ancestry, became actors as soon as they could talk. We may still see a play-bill for the year 1767—*Charles I.*—with Mr. and Mrs. Kemble, Miss Kemble (aged twelve), Master Kemble (aged ten), Miss Fanny Kemble (aged nine), and Mr. Siddons in the cast. Travelling about England with a repertory company, going "on the circuit" as it was called, seemed to them the natural, jolly, homely way of living. Among their infant memories were those of sitting quietly in dark playhouses watching the family act the stories they knew so well. It was no labour to boys and girls brought up in this way to learn Shakespearean parts, for by constant listening they had memorized them involuntarily in the same way that less fortunate children absorb fairy-tales and nursery rhymes.

At one time Roger Kemble's family appeared to pervade the British stage and threatened to dominate it. John was a conspicuous actor-manager; Sarah a supreme artist; Elizabeth, a caricature of Sarah, people said, was married to an actor-manager, Whitlock, and played before George Washington in America; Stephen was first an actor in London and later manager at Edinburgh; Fanny, an actress, was married to an actor-manager; Henry was on the stage; two other sisters acted in minor rôles at Drury Lane; and lastly Charles, "whose looks Apollo might have envied", captivated all hearts as the perfect lover. And it was not in London only that the Kembles were known; there was not a theatre of any standing in the provinces at which one or other of them did not from time to time appear.

Mrs. Siddons, the Sarah mentioned above, had begun her London career under Garrick's management at Drury Lane and was re-engaged by Sheridan when he took charge of the theatre. Her greatest successes were scored when playing with her brother John in *Henry VIII.* and *Macbeth.* So great a 'Queen Katharine' had never been seen by mortal man, nor so terrible a 'Lady Macbeth'. Crowds surged through the Piazza when she was to act. As a tiny girl her niece, Fanny Kemble, looked down from a window on a mob of heads and then was carried off to a box to see her fat and rather alarming aunt transformed into 'Lady Randolph' at one of her last appearances upon the stage.

Fanny's childhod was steeped in legends of her famous relations. There had been a great day for the family in 1794, shortly after the theatre had been re-built, when *Macbeth* was presented at Drury Lane. Uncle John and Aunt Sarah had played the leading parts, her own father had been 'Malcolm' and other aunts and uncles had hovered in the background eager to participate in this intimate success. No tragedienne had ever been so much admired as Aunt Sarah. In the hey-day of her triumph the "chariots of the nobility" had besieged her lodgings in the Strand; the King and Dr. Johnson had both paid her marked attention; the gentlemen of Brooks' had made her a handsome gift; Burke, Gibbon, Fox, and Reynolds had sat in the stalls enthralled by her acting, and had all paid homage to her behind the scenes. Story after story of old successes was poured into the alert ears of the Kemble children.

In the course of time "magnificent-looking" John Kemble became part lessee and manager of Covent Garden, and stalked through all his great parts— 'Hamlet', 'King Lear,' 'Coriolanus', 'Brutus', 'Cato'— with that monotonous dignity and strange diction which his admirers thought very wonderful. The classical characters were those in which he excelled, and he contemplated himself in them with such satisfaction that after a time, imbued with the virtues of 'Coriolanus', he made no effort to shake himself free of Roman manners in private life. Washington Irving, who saw him act 'Othello' in 1805, wrote home disappointed with his cold, majestic stage manner, and commented on the absence of rich bass tones in his voice. Some people were ungracious enough to carp at his pronunciation of such words as odious, hideous, perfidious, which in his mouth were transformed into "ojus", "hijjus", "perfijjus". Virtue was transformed to "varchue" and aches became "aitches". No such criticisms were levelled at Mrs. Siddons. Washington Irving could not speak too strongly of the effect she produced on him; he "could hardly move when she was on the stage", she "froze her audience". Even iconoclastic Leigh Hunt found her "mistress of appalling tragic effect".

Perhaps the story told by Macready's father, himself an actor, gives one the truest idea of Mrs. Siddons' power. He went with his friend Holman to the pit for the performance of *Tamerlane*. John Kemble was playing 'Bajazet'; Mrs. Siddons, 'Aspasia'; and Charles Kemble, 'Monesis'. In the last act, when 'Aspasia's' lover

'Monesis' is strangled before her face, Mrs. Siddons worked herself up to such a pitch of agony, and gave such terrible reality to the few convulsive words she tried to utter as she sank in a lifeless heap before his murderers, that the audience remained for a few moments in a hush of astonishment as if awestruck; they then clamoured for the curtain to be dropped and, insisting on the manager's appearance, received from him, in answer to their vehement inquiries, the assurance that Mrs. Siddons was alive. They would not suffer the performance to be resumed. Holman turned to his friend and said: "Macready, do I look as pale as you?"

The year of Fanny's birth, 1809, saw the reopening of Covent Garden after the fire. Once more "the family" made an impressive appearance in *Macbeth*, playing the same parts as they had done fifteen years earlier at Drury Lane. Already they had become a tradition.

One thinks of Fanny set against this background of ancestral figures as of a child in the presence of spectres. They were always there with their mannerisms, their fame, and their triumphs. To follow in such footsteps must have seemed as difficult a task as for a pygmy to emulate the stride of giants. Though unvoiced family pressure pushed her towards the footlights, she was slow to recognize the power of its compulsion and contentedly spun the fabric of her life out of any material that drifted her way. Among the strands that came into her hands we catch a glimpse of twinkling, transatlantic filaments that at first served to brighten and beautify life, but in the end wove the shroud of her delight.

We may trace some of them, light as gossamers, floating into the lives of her parents. A letter carried by Washington Irving to Mademoiselle Decamp of Covent Garden from Mrs. Johnson of the Park Theatre, New York, which elicited an invitation to her house and brought about a meeting with Charles Kemble, a kind visit from Mrs. Van Wart, Irving's sister, acquaintance with Peter Irving, a meeting with John Howard Payne, friendship with the Brevoorts. One after another these links with America accumulated until there was formed an invisible chain compact of familiarity, neighbourliness and mutual benefit. Sympathy in misfortune strengthened the bond when Washington and Peter Irving became bankrupt, and Payne a prisoner for debt in London.

One of the great theatrical hits of 1818 was *Brutus* or *The Fall of the Tarquins*, produced at Drury Lane, with Stephen Kemble as stage manager and Henry Kemble playing Sextus. It had a run of fifty-three nights which at that time was considered remarkable. Creditors pursued the author, John Howard Payne, vigorously, thinking he must be coining money. After taking what he had, they committed him to prison till he could discharge all his debts. Extricating himself by the adaptation of a musical play, *Thérèse* (sold promptly to Elliston, the manager of Drury Lane), he fled to Paris, the refuge of the financially embarrassed, and consorted there with Tom Moore and the Irvings, who were as short of cash as himself.

Teresa or *The Orphan of Geneva* was produced with

such success at Drury Lane in 1821 that Charles Kemble, when he took over his brother's interest in Covent Garden in 1822, at once began to negotiate with Payne in the hope of persuading him to desert the rival play-house. Elliston was "inert enough" to lose Payne's services, and Charles Kemble wasted no time in securing *Clari* or *The Maid of Milan*. This play contained a song that took the town by storm. "Home sweet Home" was whistled from the Strand to the banks of the Ohio. The theatre was packed nightly and the management raked in some thousands of pounds. Flushed with excitement over this lucky venture, Kemble begged the American author to hunt up more plays for him at once. Payne was pleased to agree, but only by obtaining assistance could he comply with the demand. Hurrying to Paris he discussed with Washington Irving the possibilities of immediately submitting further adaptations to the Covent Garden syndicate, with the result that the two men there and then agreed to work in partnership.

Some prejudice against the stage must have existed in Irving's mind, for he would not allow his name to appear as collaborator, though he agreed to do half the work and take half the profits. Ten years later this prejudice had evaporated, and his name appears in a Drury Lane play-bill as author of *The Alchymist*. We find this reluctance to have anything to do with the theatre in others of that day. For example, Leigh Hunt, though he wrote "Theatricals" for his brother's paper, *The News*, at one time thought it "a sin to know an actor personally", and would "as lief have taken poison as have accepted a ticket from the theatre".

Whatever the reason for this reluctance to associate his name with the writing of plays, Irving had no objection to hard work, and the two friends sat down in a sky parlour of the Palais Royale to experiment with *La Jeunesse de Richelieu* and *La Jeunesse d'Henri V.* by Alexandre Duval. When *Richelieu* and a French farce were complete Payne set off covertly for London to market them, while Irving continued in Paris busy transforming *Henry V.* into *Charles II.*

The collaborators devised a definite plan of co-operation. Payne first did the donkey work of literal translation, then Irving re-wrote the dialogue and indicated the places in which songs or choruses should be inserted, and then Payne went over it again from the technical point of view. The method adopted becomes clear when Irving says of *Azendai* that he read Payne's translation and noted where alterations should be made and songs introduced. Finding the dialogue "flimsy and pointless" he re-wrote it, but the main thing—the construction was serviceable and needed no pulling about.

Irving in due course transmitted *Charles II.* and *Azendai* to London, and Payne, in acknowledging the safe receipt of the manuscripts, wrote that in his opinion *Charles II.* was "one of the best pieces of the kind he had ever read, a never diminishing stream of wit and eminently dramatic situations". Like *Clari*, it contained a song that caught the popular fancy and delighted Charles Lamb.

In the time of the Rump
As old Admiral Trump
With his broom swept the chaps of the Channel
And his crew of Big Breeches
Those Dutch sons of . . . .

It went to a swinging lilt, and the joke of it—Irving's joke, by the way—was that the singer, Captain Copp, was never allowed to finish "the horrible, rough song", for his niece Mary clapped her hand over his mouth at the critical moment. Washington Irving went with Payne and his great friend Mary Shelley to the second night's performance. They were all delighted with the success of the piece.

After prolonged bargaining, Charles Kemble paid two hundred guineas for *Richelieu* and *Charles II*. Payne knew no better way of acknowledging his secret debt of gratitude than to dedicate *Charles II*. to his collaborator.

Meanwhile, in London, a young English actor, John Kerr, thought to dramatize *Rip Van Winkle*. It was given at the West London Theatre in 1825, four years before it was played in America. Washington Irving and Payne were among the first-night audience. It seems probable that Irving with his eager interest in things theatrical may have assisted John Kerr to dramatize his own story, possibly for the sake of securing copyright fees. This appears to be the first original American play produced in England. Though Americans had worked for some time for the English stage, and had even imported a negro Othello, there was

nothing characteristically American about the pot-
boilers concocted by Payne and Irving in Paris.

§ II

The Charles Kembles moved house almost as frequently as strollers. Sometimes they were to be found
in the Piazza, Covent Garden, sometimes by Paddington Churchyard or among the elms at Craven Hill,
sometimes in Soho or Westminster. Mrs. Kemble, who
loved trees and fields and rivers, made the four children
the excuse for having a cottage at Weybridge, to which
she could repair when her husband was on tour and
where she could indulge her passion for fishing. She
was an attractive, witty woman, and Charles was an
important stage personality, so in the natural course of
events interesting people drifted in and out of their
lives with the pleasant informality bred of common
interests. Mario, Talma, Reynolds were among them.
Chantrey was a "frequenter". Weber, when he came
over to superintend the first production of the *Freischütz* at Covent Garden, was constantly in their house.
The young Kembles heard the music till they knew it
by heart, and Fanny, who never did things by halves,
bought a small engraving of the composer, folded it up
and sewed it into a black silk case, which she wore like
a scapular round her neck. When Sir George Smart,
the conductor of the Covent Garden orchestra, brought
Herr Carl Maria von Weber to the Kemble's house for

FANNY KEMBLE

Aged 20

From a drawing by Sir Thomas Lawrence

the first time, he presented him formally to Fanny, saying: "All the young girls are in love with you, sir". Fanny blushed and, thinking guiltily of her pendant, stammered out something about loving his music. "My music!" exclaimed the composer wearily; "it is always my music, never myself."

The *Freischütz* had such an immense success at Covent Garden that it was put on at nine provincial theatres simultaneously. Fired by the hope of striking another gold mine, Charles Kemble commissioned Weber to write an opera for him. The theme chosen was Wieland's *Oberon*, and Weber, much pleased, went back to Dresden to work at the score. In April 1826 he reappeared with his new music, and the opera was put into rehearsal. While waiting for its production he conducted repetitions of the *Freischütz* before packed houses. Fanny Kemble who saw him frequently, describes him as "a little thin man and lame, with hook nose, sallow face, high cheek-bones and light prominent eyes". Though ill at the time, he overworked himself at rehearsals, and was terribly cast down when on the opening night *Oberon* was not received with the furore he had hoped for. Artists are temperamental in a high degree, and it was almost unbearable that sleek Rossini should arrive in London just at the time *Oberon* was produced, and that the fickle public should swarm round the newcomer. Weber, "feeling himself in a desert", took to his bed and died almost suddenly at the house of Sir George Smart in Great Portland Street. Fanny Kemble received a lock of his hair; the well-worn scapular had fallen to pieces just before his death.

In spite of the success of *Clari, Charles II.*, and the *Freischütz*, Charles Kemble could not make Covent Garden pay. He had no particular commercial ability himself, though he was apt to drive hard bargains with authors and provincial managers. He was also hampered by having, in Fawcett, a most inefficient stage-manager. Covent Garden was not, however, a fair test for anyone, for its proprietors were at loggerheads suing each other, its patents of doubtful validity, and its building encumbrances heavy. The first serious crisis arose in 1827 when one of the proprietors saw fit to throw the whole business into Chancery. The case came before Lord Eldon, Lord Brougham, and Sir John Leach. Fanny went with her father to listen to the proceedings, and came away rather downcast after the judges had arrived at a decision that, in consequence of debts encumbering the property, Charles Kemble, as part owner, was liable at any time to be called on to produce twenty-seven thousand pounds. Without private capital, unable to disentangle himself from his contract with the syndicate or sell his share in the theatre, he had to carry on as best he could in management and make money for his family by playing Shakespearean parts at the Salle Favart in Paris and by provincial tours in Great Britain. Every leading player at this time looked to his "annual promenade" through the country to bring him in four or five times as much as that of a London engagement.

Mrs. Charles Kemble, who, from the age of twelve, had assisted to support her mother, looked at her own children to see what help could be expected from them. None of the four had shown any aptitude for the stage, though Fanny spent many hours in writing plays. The girl certainly had brains, but could she act? It was strange that she should never have shown any wish to do so. They had given her a good education at schools in France and England. She could talk and read French, German, and Italian. Her taste in books was serious: she preferred the works of Dante, Goethe, Tieck, Wieland, and Sismondi to those of other writers; still she knew whole scenes from Racine and Corneille by heart, as well as complete Shakespearean parts; how could it be that she felt no impulse to act them? Obviously there must be a strong Puritan strain running through the younger generation. How else could one account for a daughter who read dull books and a son who longed to become a clergyman? In spite of the maturity of her mind Fanny seemed to her mother almost a child, so completely lacking was she in vanity and in dramatic sense. Was she really wanting in these qualities or were they merely undeveloped? Mrs. Kemble pondered over these things and consulted her sister, Adelaide Decamp, as to what should be done. After all, they had both worked from childhood up, and as juvenile stage dancers in the Le Texier troupe had been petted by Mrs. Fitzherbert and the Prince Regent. Madame Decamp had trained them to be practical cooks and dressmakers, and Mrs.

Kemble could not remember the time when she had not been occupied either in making her own stage clothes, adapting French farces to British taste, or concocting jujubes for actors' throats. These children of hers seemed lazy by comparison; they did nothing but read, an unprofitable pursuit. What was to be done about it, and why in the name of fortune should Fanny have offered to become a governess? How would that help the family? Surely the child must realize that financial help was expected of her, and yet she made no sign of understanding. Adelaide Decamp, "dear Aunt Dall", as the young people called her, advised patience. Fanny should be left to her own devices. In good time something would happen.

One day in the autumn of 1829, Charles Kemble being absent on a professional tour in Ireland, his wife dropped into a chair in her little Pimlico drawing-room and burst into tears. "It has come at last", she sobbed to Fanny, "our property is to be sold. I have seen that fine building all covered with placards and bills of sale: the theatre must be closed and I know not how many people cut adrift from employment." Fanny, on whom there had at last begun to dawn what was expected of her, showed practical sense and at once recited 'Portia's' great speech. Her mother mopped her eyes and listened intently. "There is hardly passion enough in the part to test any tragic power," she said. "I wish you would study 'Juliet' for me." A day or two later Fanny went through the part of 'Juliet'. Mrs. Kemble again listened with keen attention, but made no observation of any kind.

When Charles Kemble returned from Ireland, Fanny very nervously recited the parts again before both parents. They did not seem dissatisfied, and a few days later her voice was tried in the holland-coated theatre, where a spot-light from above picked her out from the surrounding gloom. "I acted 'Juliet' as I do not believe I ever acted it again to any visible 'Romeo'," wrote Fanny afterwards.

Sitting hidden at the back of a box was an old friend, the only spectator. His advice, "Bring her out at once; she will be a great success", was acted on. After three weeks' intensive coaching by her mother she appeared as 'Juliet', in the traditional low-cut white satin dress with a long train. She wore a girdle of paste brilliants round her waist and a comb of brilliants in her hair. "The theatre dresser performed my toilet, and at length I was placed in a chair with satin train laid carefully over the back of it and tears brimming over rouged cheeks."

Though sixteen years had elapsed since Mrs. Charles Kemble had acted, she determined to play 'Lady Capulet' in order to welcome her extremely frightened daughter to the stage. They were to enter from opposite sides, and, as Fanny waited in the wings, she heard someone say to her: "The people in the stalls are nothing but a row of cabbages, Miss Fanny—a row of cabbages that is how one should regard them". When the call "Juliet!" sounded she rushed on to the stage and clung to her mother. After the first paralysing moment her breeding came to her rescue and she acted "in a frenzy of passion and entire self-forgetfulness".

Aunt Sarah sat in a little recess or box specially fitted up for her opposite the prompter, and cried with joy and tried to remember how she had acted at her own first appearance in London fifty-five years earlier. Would this niece of hers carry on the great Kemble tradition? It almost seemed possible, for the house was wild with enthusiasm. It was a pity, of course, that she was so squat and that the smallpox had so muddied her complexion, but in spite of disadvantages she had the Kemble manner, voice and intonation combined with the gaiety of youth, good teeth, lovely eyes, and great intelligence. Perhaps she might pull the family fortunes round; this was to be hoped, as poor Charles was on the verge of bankruptcy.

Washington Irving joined in the stunning applause that greeted Fanny's first appearance. Supping later that evening with her parents, she found a gold watch on her plate—a gift from a doting father. Irving came in to supplement his claps with personal congratulations. Snatching up the watch he held it to his ear and then with mock surprise exclaimed: "Why, it goes!" The Kembles were in a mood to laugh at anything that night, and the joke was greeted with a roar. Then they fell to discussing the performance. There was no doubt of Fanny's triumph; they must drink the child's health. With a salary fixed at thirty pounds a week by the management, Fanny felt very rich and important. Strange that one evening could make so great a difference in one's life.

Henceforward, she played 'Juliet' three times a week.

There were no rehearsals to attend, for the booking for *Romeo and Juliet* gave promise that it would carry on through the season. From being a dowdy girl dressing on twenty pounds a year and hesitating whether she could afford to hail an omnibus, she suddenly became the owner of fine clothes, a riding horse, a carriage. She bought handsome presents for all the family. It certainly was great fun to be a success.

Mrs. Kemble took care that her daughter led a quiet, regular life so as to be fresh for her work. After dining "in the middle of the day on a mutton chop", she was taken by Aunt Dall to the theatre. All the time she was not acting she sat in her dressing-room working at tapestry or needlework. Aunt Dall carried her train when she was called for the stage, and remained in the wings to gather it up again after the performance and to throw a shawl round her shoulders. No visits to the green-room were permitted for fear of distraction. It was impressed on Fanny that Talma, in order to think himself into his parts, dressed two hours before he was expected on the stage. Fanny's poise was wonderful and her vogue fantastic. On some days the house rose to greet her, and as she added Aunt Sarah's parts, 'Belvidera' and 'Euphrasia', to her repertory, she became to countless young men and women an object of adoration. Certain persons, Sir Thomas Lawrence, Lord Wilton, and a clergyman, son of William IV., hardly ever missed a performance. The newspapers extolled the young actress; souvenir plates and mugs appeared painted with pictures of her as 'Juliet', 'Belvidera', and other heroines. Gentlemen pulled out silk handkerchiefs spotted with lilac flowers which on close examination turned out to be minute likenesses of Fanny's head.

§ III

Sir Thomas Lawrence's connection with the Kemble family was of long standing and interwoven with tragedy. Twenty years earlier he had become engaged to Mrs. Siddons' daughter, Maria, "beautiful as a seraph". Her "clever and elegant" sister, Sarah, supplanted her. One day a letter for the new love fell into the hand of the old. From that moment Maria drooped, sickened, and then died. On her death-bed she exacted a promise from Sarah that she would never marry Lawrence. In conformity with the strange anæmic fashion of her day, Sarah too pined and after a while expired. After this double loss, Mrs. Siddons banished the philanderer from her house and mind.

It was an old story; the wounding edge had become blunt, and Charles Kemble was not affronted when Lawrence accosted him in the street just after his girl's first appearance on the stage, to beg permission to pay his respects to Mrs. Kemble and make the acquaintance of Miss Fanny. Charming in looks and bearing, he was said to resemble Canning, Fanny was flattered by the attention he paid her. Early memories stirred within him as he watched the girl. "Might I make a drawing of the child? She is like Sarah, she is like Maria, she is like them all," he murmured. Mrs. Kemble acquiesced, and took Fanny to sit to him in the long picture gallery at his house. He made a drawing of head and shoulders, and presented it to Mrs. Kemble; it is probably the last drawing he ever made. Soon this sketch was reproduced, every shop window showing copies of it. Sir Thomas appointed a day on which to commence a full-length portrait of Fanny as 'Juliet', but died before he could begin work on it.

On her twentieth birthday Fanny had received from him a proof plate of Sir Joshua Reynold's picture of Mrs. Siddons as 'The Tragic Muse'. It was inscribed: "This portrait by England's greatest painter of the noblest subject of his pencil is presented to her niece and worthy successor by her most faithful, humble servant and friend, Lawrence". His devotion took the form of watching her attentively every time she acted, and of writing her notes embodying praise or criticism. He wanted her to act even better than she did, and being a man of sixty he could remember enough of Mrs. Siddons' ways to give her hints and help as to the family tradition. Fanny came to depend on these faithful suggestions and adjust her gesture or inflection in accordance with his advice. Though his manner to all women was that of a courtly lover, his life, so far as love itself was concerned, had been a failure; Fanny called up in him something of his former romances. On the last occasion he saw her, he put into her hand a first edition of *Paradise Lost*, which may or may not have been symbolic.

Mrs. Charles Kemble had found him invaluable as an

arbiter for clothes for the stage. It was difficult to know just how to dress a young girl for the old, well-known parts, as the conception of theatrical costume was changing rapidly in the direction of archaeological accuracy. Gone was the time in which it was permissible to act 'Macbeth', as Garrick did, in satin coat, knee-breeches, and powdered wig. Fanny, of course, could not wear the dresses improvised by the elder generation. Why! when Aunt Sarah had first played 'Euphrasia' in *The Grecian Daughter* her hair was dressed in powdered curls surmounted by a forest of feathers and she wore a hoop and high-heeled shoes, but somehow both she and Garrick could make any audience believe that they looked just as they should. When Fanny played 'Euphrasia' she wore "a pseudo-Greek confection consisting of a full white skirt, a long train with a rich gold Grecian border, a fine white merino peplum beautifully embroidered, leaving my arms quite free and uncovered save by long flesh-coloured gloves". A bright scarlet sash with a heavy gold fringe completed a costume which was the evident pride of its wearer. As 'Belvidera', in *Venice Preserved*, Lawrence, who hated to see the girl in mourning, though he had worn mourning for twenty years himself, reluctantly agreed to let her wear a plain black velvet dress with a black hat and white feather before the crisis, and after the betrayal a lugubrious long black veil.

One evening Fanny was sitting in her dressing-room at the theatre, re-reading some of Sir Thomas's letters, ready to go on in this part, when her father suddenly opened the door and said shortly, "Lawrence is dead". The play went haltingly after this shock; the wonder is it went at all. Neither she nor her mother dared face the great funeral at St. Paul's. Fanny admitted to herself that perhaps his death was timely, as she was on the verge of falling in love with him. London deplored that there was no artist worthy to succeed him as President of the Royal Academy.

§ IV

Old playgoers compared Fanny with her Aunt Sarah. It seemed strange that that incomparable actress should have achieved fame so much more painfully than her niece. It was called to mind that when Mrs. Siddons originally appeared in London as 'Portia', a frightened, tottering, badly-dressed figure had spoken the verses in a hurried whisper, and had only pulled itself together in time to deliver the famous speech audibly and correctly. Her emergence from the provinces had brought her perilously near failure, though she had plenty of acting experience. How was it that Fanny, aged twenty, with no experience whatever of the stage, should suddenly rise by nature, not by art, to be a star of the first magnitude?

Charles Greville had to admit that Mrs. Siddons was not so good at her age, but he did not admire "the new Kemble". In his diary he wrote her down as "short and ill-made, with large hands and feet". As an amateur of women he could not allow that she was handsome, but merely that her countenance was expressive; her voice he thought good, but he detected in it "a little of the drawl of her family". In sophisticated Greville she excited no emotion, but he admitted that as she was very young and clever, "it was possible she might become a good, possibly a fine actress". He noted that she filled the house every night.

That was the important thing about her from her parents' point of view; she did fill the house, and, if applause was any criterion, she did please almost everyone. On the strength of Fanny's success the family moved to a good house in Great Russell Street, and passers-by in Russell Square could often see a little figure pacing up and down learning new parts. As the receipts poured in at the theatre, the Charles Kembles began to hope that with two or three years of hard work they might get enough money together to retire and live in the south of France, for in quite a short time Fanny had enabled her father to pay off thirteen thousand pounds of debt. Uncle John had already set the example of living abroad; he had carried off his savings to Lausanne, where he made a home for his old age. People who saw him there said he was jealous of Mont Blanc for attracting more attention from tourists than he did.

Some girls would have had their heads turned by success and flattery, but Fanny seemed to remain the same simple little person who had once played at dolls' dinners on the flat tombstones of Paddington churchyard and spent days on the river bank at Weybridge putting worms on hooks for her mother. But when all was said and done the stage held no illusions for her; she had been mixed up with it all her life, and probably no applause would ever impress her so much as the frightful clapping she had heard accorded to Aunt Sarah when she was a child of seven. The Kembles were accustomed as a family to histrionic triumphs; failure would have been far more upsetting. Even her social success Fanny took quietly, though it was the very pinnacle of fun to be young and popular in London. Her spare evenings were "bespoke". Sometimes it was a dinner with Lord Melbourne or a ball at Devonshire House, sometimes a rout at the house of nonagenarian Lady Cork, where the hostess appeared as a little witch bride dressed in white satin, white bonnet and veil. Chairs were clamped to the walls at these parties to make *tête-à-tête* impossible. Then her older admirers, Rogers, Campbell, Tom Moore, Washington Irving, would give parties for her. She soon got used to being in crowded rooms and to "being much stared at".

Her brothers' friends, young and delightful, clustered round her: Arthur Hallam, Alfred Tennyson, John Sterling, Richard Monckton Milnes, William Thackeray, Edward Fitzgerald, Frederick Maurice, she knew them all. "We were all of us in love with you," said Thackeray years later, "and had your portrait by Lawrence in our rooms."

§ v

George Stephenson was one of the "lions" of 1830. Fanny fell "horribly in love" with him. In his north-country burr he told her to be sure to come and ride on his new railway when she and her father went on their circuit to Manchester and Liverpool. In August 1830 she had her ride, and on the way Stephenson told her the story of his great experiment which had been turned down by the Government Committee appointed to investigate its merits and subsequently financed by a group of local merchants. To be made a confidant of by "the greatest of living inventors" was a matter of great pride to Fanny. A month later she and her parents were staying with the Wiltons at Heaton Park for the formal opening of the Liverpool-Manchester Railway. Eight hundred persons were stowed into the train, which moved between dense walls of cheering people. Fanny was screwed up to the pitch of exhilaration, imagining the delight of always travelling in this smooth, swift way instead of lumbering along dusty roads in a stage-coach. Her reflections were interrupted by a halt. It was said in a joking fashion that the "iron horse" needed a drink, and presently it sped past the window in quest of one, at what seemed to Fanny lightning pace. Some people got down from the carriages and stood on the track; the Duke of Wellington and his political enemy, Mr. Huskisson, the member for Liverpool, among them. The iron horse whizzed back to duty, but moments went by, and the train did not move. Presently a report circulated among the passengers that an accident had occurred. Fanny looked out of window and there, surely enough, she saw poor Mr. Huskisson lying on the ground with a severed artery, and Lord Wilton, her host, kneeling on the track beside him trying to stanch the blood.

Everyone was much upset, and the Duke of Wellington tried to cancel the rest of the programme, but was told the whole population of Manchester was waiting to welcome the train, and proceed he must. The journey finished glumly. Late that night Mr. Huskisson died. Fanny was glad to get away from the memory of this catastrophe and to resume work. She and her father continued their theatrical tour to Glasgow and Edinburgh, and Fanny had the great felicity of breakfasting with her adored Sir Walter Scott. His daughter Anne and Miss Ferrier, author of the novels *Marriage* and *Inheritance*, were also present. The great man was cordial, even affectionate, and Fanny enshrined her talk with him amongst her most treasured memories.

From Scotland they proceeded to Ireland, where all the Kembles had in their day scored great successes. Fanny kept up the tradition. When she stepped out of the stage door in Dublin after playing in *The Fair Penitent*, she found a bodyguard of two hundred young men cheering her, and before escorting her back to the hotel they all dropped down on one knee to peep under her bonnet. Touring was both amusing and advantageous to Charles Kemble. He took Fanny all over England. At one time or another they acted at Bath,

Plymouth, Exeter, Portsmouth, Southampton, and even Weymouth, where, in the little theatre beloved of George III. and Queen Charlotte, Fanny's mother had acted before her and had been given coral beads by the Princess Amelia. There was hardly a playhouse in the realm in which members of the Kemble family had not appeared, and old playgoers were always turning up who remembered them all.

Among the acquaintances made by Fanny in London were Lord and Lady Francis Leveson Gower who lived at Bridgewater House. Lady Francis became an intimate and adored friend, always eager to carry Fanny off for week-ends at Oatlands. Lord Francis, who had translated *Faust*, had also made a rhymed translation of *Hernani* which he longed to produce privately. If he rigged up a stage at Bridgewater House, would Fanny, he asked, act the lead 'Donna Sol'? It was rather an amusing idea to her to be the only professional in an amateur cast, and she agreed. The rehearsals wasted a great deal of time, but the company was pulled together at last and gave a tolerable performance. The chairs were extremely close to the stage, and on the night Fanny found herself declaiming right into the face of the Archbishop of Canterbury. A month later the play was repeated for the Queen, but the super-genteel Court audience was a poor public to play to, especially as no applause was allowed in the presence of royalty. After the performance Fanny was presented to the Queen, Princess Elizabeth, and the Duke of Gloucester. It was all very amusing for once in a while, but heaven forfend that she should take part in amateur theatricals again. There was work enough to do in studying characters professionally without adding to it by profitless amiability. It was the custom for leading actors and actresses to do little more at rehearsals than read or repeat the words of their parts, marking on them their entrances and exits as settled by the stage manager, and their respective places on the scene. With amateurs the rehearsals were prolonged and numerous and the results achieved exceedingly small. Fanny turned away thankfully to work at new parts and soon added 'Beatrice' in *Much Ado about Nothing*, 'Constance' in *King John*, 'Mrs. Beverly' in *The Gamester*, 'Bianca' in *Fazio*, 'Isabella' in *The Fatal Marriage*, 'Lady Teazle' in *The School for Scandal*, to her original stock-in-trade. In the last scene of *The Gamester*, when 'Beverly' is dying of self-administered poison, she could always work up a terrible effect not only on the audience but on herself. Charles Kemble sometimes had to carry 'Mrs. Beverly' to the dressing-room, where she would scream for five minutes before releasing herself from her impersonation. People who saw her in every rôle said she was at her best as 'Julia' in *The Hunchback*, a play specially written for her by Sheridan Knowles, in which he played the name part. It was the most popular original play of the day, on both sides of the Atlantic. Audiences were delighted to be able to laugh at Fanny as a fine, affected young woman of fashion, and to assist at evolving a happy marriage plot instead of leaving the theatre horror-struck by the vision of bloody ghosts as in *Venice Preserved*, or plunged in tears over the suicide of a gambler.

A young American visitor to London, Mr. James Handasyd Perkins, wrote to his family in Cincinnati saying he had seen Miss Kemble act once and meant to go every time she played, "even if he had to pawn his last shirt to buy a seat". "I have a ticket for next Monday night when she plays 'Constance' in *King John*. It is her benefit, and the tickets (boxes and dress circle) are all signed by her. I will give you an autograph . . . it deserves to be kept as a valuable legacy. . . . She is a very beautiful girl. . . . I should wish to be moderate in what I say in praise of her, and so I think if anything will ever tempt me to cross the Atlantic again it will be the hope of seeing Fanny Kemble."

Charles Greville was present at the first performance of Fanny's own tragedy, *Francis I.*, and pronounced it "a complete success". To the author, who acted in it, the lines appeared trite and dull. Ten editions of the play had been sold by John Murray before it was produced, and the gratified author had received a cheque for four hundred and fifty pounds, with which she bought a commission for her brother Henry.

When Mrs. Siddons died in January 1831, Covent Garden was closed for a week. "I could wish 'Lady Macbeth' be not played for ten years in honour of my aunt," sighed Fanny, knowing that she was about to be called on by her father to study the part, for the family tradition could not be allowed to lapse.

No amount of hard work on the part of the Kembles,

however, could make Covent Garden a solvent, secure business enterprise. What use was it to pay off building debts on the property if the very patents on which it was held were worth nothing? When the Chancery Court during the winter of 1831–32 gave a decision of invalidity of patent, the Kembles had to abandon all hope of pulling the place round. "If I had £10,000 a year," exclaimed happy-go-lucky Charles Kemble, "I could have saved it." His wife and daughter stared at him. After all they had been through they would not have spent another farthing in propping up the bankrupt concern.

The last performance under his management took place in March. Fanny appeared as Julia before a crowded house. When taking her last curtain she snatched a nosegay from her sash and tossed it over the footlights with a handful of kisses. It had been "our theatre" after all, and this was the end. Friends clustered round Charles Kemble, anxious to advise and possibly to help. John Howard Payne, who was on the point of returning to his native land, told Kemble that American theatrical tours often proved very lucrative. Washington Irving re-enforced this statement and Stephen Price, the American lessee of Drury Lane, offered to arrange 'a circuit' in the United States.

Price, a bluff fellow and a gambler, whose betting-book for Epsom and Ascot was made up for him by Gully the pugilist, was the first of the American managers to come to London. He knew nothing of dramatic literature, but he had an instinct that if only he could

give the public what it wanted any theatre must pay.
He was sure America would like to see the Kembles,
and so persuaded Charles to enter into an agreement
to perform there for two years. The advantages of
being out of the way of creditors and in the way of
making a fortune were too obvious to be missed, and,
after combating his daughter's tearful objections to
leaving home, Charles Kemble signed articles to Price
binding him to appear in New York and other cities
in the autumn of 1832. An offer on the part of Aunt
Dall to accompany Fanny was jumped at. By this
means some of the dear home atmosphere might be
preserved and the inevitable strangeness of life in
America tempered. "Good-bye, my world of England," sobbed Fanny as she sailed for the country in
which fate lay waiting for her.

§ VI

"I have led a loathsome life in the ship for a month
past," wrote the traveller in her diary, "and yet the last
Saturday night seemed half sad. . . . We danced on
deck; the sky was like the jewel shop of the angels. . . ."
What "foul nonsense" it was to be sentimental at
parting with a ship's company one did not even like,
but somehow unreasoning regrets started to life un-
bidden, and tears flowed even when one should be
rejoicing at the first sight of New York, "with its
clustered lights shining like a distant constellation
against the dark outline of the land".

A schooner came alongside the *Pacific*, giving latest news of the cholera in Boston. The epidemic had passed through New York, and the Park and Bowery theatres had been closed for two months. Now that it had subsided, places of amusement were once more open. Next morning in a warm, clinging fog the ladies of the party donned pelisses and bonnets and were put ashore by a steamship. Houses painted red or white and green-shuttered were dimly to be discerned, and trees giving a garden-like effect. A hackney coach deposited them at the "American Hotel". Fanny, feeling "dreadfully depressed", pounced on a piano and played and sang till exhausted. In the evening their fellow-passengers dined, wined, danced, and sang in their apartment. Charles Kemble was in his element, but his daughter slipped off to bed while a guest was discoursing tipsily about the soul. It being too hot the following day to dress in "a silk pelisse", and alternative raiment being still detained in the Custom House, Fanny sat about in a dressing-gown while passengers wandered in and out making further farewells.

The hotel reminded her of the Shelbourne in "dear, dirty Dublin". Paper was peeling off the walls; beds were without curtains, sofas and chairs were shabby; everywhere there were mosquitoes and flies. The servants slept on the sofas of the public rooms. Fanny noticed that there were "no water pipes or cisterns in this city such as we have at home, but men go about as they do in Paris, with huge water-butts supplying each house daily". As always at that period it was necessary to go to a bathing establishment to obtain a bath. There were three or four bath-houses in New York at that time, "mainly supported by foreigners". A male traveller of that time observed: "Though the English despise the comforts of the bath, they cannot have a greater practical contempt for it than the Americans".

Charles Kemble was surprised at the cost of rooms, food, and wine. With champagne and claret at eleven shillings, and sherry, port, and madeira at nine shillings to thirteen shillings a bottle, a party was an expensive luxury. The family would have to be niggardly till the theatre opened and salaries were paid.

While waiting for her luggage to arrive Fanny did nothing but look out of the window "all the blessed day long. I did not think in my old age to acquire so Jezebel a trick; but the park is so very pretty and the streets so gay with their throngs of smartly dressed women. . . . The women dress like French women gone mad."

Up and down Broadway ran "omnibuses of rank": "Lady Clinton", "Lady Washington", and "Lady Van Rennslaer", rattled their crazy bones along the pavement. There were also swinging coaches all complete with hammer-cloth, coachman and footmen. Misled by these relics of another dispensation, she wrote: "'Tis my conviction America will be a monarchy before I am a skeleton". Baskets of camellias, tuberoses, and violets were brought to her room. Welcoming strangers called. Everyone spoke to her about *Domestic Manners of the*

Americans. "Mercy on me," she wrote, "how sore all these people are about Mrs. Trollope's book and how glad I am I did not read it. She must have spoken the truth though, for lies do not rankle so."

Charles Kemble called on Mr. Philip Hone, a prominent citizen, whom we now know as the author of an amusing diary, and presented letters of introduction from Mr. Vaughan, British Minister in Washington, and Mr. Price. On returning the call Mr. Hone found Fanny alone. She appeared to him sprightly, easy-mannered, intelligent, but not very handsome, and he thought it possible people might dislike her on first acquaintance, as her manners were "somewhat singular".

Presently twenty huge boxes were delivered untouched by the Customs. Fanny and her father rapidly changed into cool clothes and went off to see Wallack in *The Rent Day*, a melodrama by Douglas Jerrold. The Park Theatre was decorated with gold carving and red silk, and seemed to be about the size of the Haymarket in London. Fanny looked about inquisitively, for in a fortnight she and her father would be occupying that same stage, as Aunt Whitlock and Aunt Hatton had done before them. Manners were not elegant: men wore their hats in the pit and even in private boxes, and there was but a sprinkling of women. The scenes in *The Rent Day* reminded her of David Wilkie's pictures and made her feel homesick. When Wallack asked his wife if she would go with him to America Fanny broke down. Just before the last lines were spoken a man moved from his place. "I beg your pardon, sir," said Wallack from the stage, "but the piece is not quite over." "Thank you, Mr. Wallack," replied the stranger, "but I've had quite enough of it."

Another night they went to the Bowery Theatre, a large, fine, handsomely proportioned building with a brazen eagle on its pediment. Opened but six years earlier as a fashionable playhouse, it was soon destined, as the tide of "ton" moved westwards, to be abandoned to a less exclusive public.

These diversions over, Fanny and Aunt Dall began to put the theatrical wardrobe in order. The business of unpacking was formidable. Fanny opened her bonnet-box nervously and found her "precious Dévy squeezed to a crush. I pulled it out, renewed and re-flowered it, and now it looks good enough *pour les thauvages*"—a little mischievous phrase that showed how her mind was working. "Bewitching canezons and pelerines" were displayed to her by a German modiste. She chose two, but such a "heathen price" was asked that she bought but one.

Aunt Dall had a busy time hearing parts gabbled over by her brother-in-law and her niece, but she never failed them in temper or attention, and much of their success is attributable to her patient, intelligent help. Fanny always said that her mother had taught her everything she knew about acting, and the fact that Aunt Dall had herself for so long been connected with the theatre was a great stand-by.

American playgoers were familiar with the Kembles' stock of plays except for *Fazio*, which had not been previously acted in the United States. There is no doubt that the breach between English and American life would have been far more marked had it not been for the repertory companies which year in and year out toured the towns with English plays and formed the taste of a public too careless to trouble to read them for their literary merits. ·

Prior to the War of Independence, plays of Shakespeare, Gay, Congreve, Dryden, Addison, Farquhar, and Otway were given in New York, Philadelphia, Williamsburg, Annapolis, Charleston, and other places. A well-known stock company like that of the Lewis Hallams had thirty dramas and twelve farces in their repertory, and was responsible for educating thousands of young people in English literature and language. The War of Independence put an end to "shows" of all sorts and gave birth to a new kind of play, patriotic and political. Most of the leading events from the Boston Tea Party to Yorktown were celebrated in this way. *Bunker Hill*, *The Fall of British Tyranny*, and *Blanche of Brandywine*, were examples of this movement; but though Lewis Hallam junior tried his best to link up the stage with national events and so give it a foothold in the new state, the legitimate drama flowed quietly back into its old channels when peace was declared, and national dramas were reserved for patriotic occasions. George Washington loved English plays. We have it on the authority of Fanny's aunt, Mrs. Whitlock, that his favourite "bespeak" was *The School for Scandal*. The Kembles' audiences were therefore familiar with classical English plays as well as with the modern productions of Knowles, Payne, and other authors. Plays usually reached New York four to six months after they had been given in London.

Elfin Mrs. David Poe had flitted from town to town as member of a stock company. With tiny frame and doe-like eyes she had played the parts of 'Violante,' 'Ophelia,' 'Cordelia,' 'Ariel,' dragging about with her two baby boys; one of them, Edgar, with the same strange untamed look he had inherited from her. It was in stage finery that they tricked her out on her death-bed in the garret behind the hostelry of the Indian Queen at Richmond, a childish figure of twenty-three.

From 1820 to 1828 the Chestnut Street Theatre, Philadelphia, boasted of the best stock company in America. It was known as "Old Drury", and played from November to April in Philadelphia and, except for a short summer vacation, the rest of the year in Baltimore. Owing to the "star" system introduced by New York theatres—a system injurious to all stock companies and abhorred of native artists—Philadelphia fell into the theatrical background and New York took the stage lead. From 1830 onwards a succession of foreign "stars" arrived from England: Edmund and Charles Kean, Charles Matthews, J. B. Booth, W. Macready, and Tyrone Power. Charles and Fanny Kemble brought up the rear, and were accorded as generous a welcome as any English actors have ever met with.

§ VII

Owing to the British Minister's letter of introduction Mr. Philip Hone tried to make the Kembles' stay in New York pleasant by taking them out riding and inviting them to dinner with his family. Mr. Hone, however, had the usual American experience of finding his new English acquaintances rather wanting in simplicity and friendliness. Charles Kemble was stiff in manner and dignified in deportment as became his reputation and his fifty-seven years, but there was something puzzling about Fanny. Why should she receive advances ungraciously and affect indifference and nonchalance when people tried to make themselves agreeable? Possibly timidity and the strangeness of her surroundings made her a little self-conscious in manner; one never knew, but she certainly was not making a good impression on the beaux. It was revealed to the Hones three years later, when Fanny was ill-advised enough to publish her *Journal*, that appearances had not belied her, and that her first reactions to open-hearted cordial America had been those of criticism and contempt.

The Kemble season at the Park Theatre opened with *Hamlet*. Fanny and Aunt Dall looked out from their box upon a crowded house. There were few ladies, but the audience was discriminating and welcoming in its applause. By some people Charles Kemble's interpretation was considered too formal, by others he was acclaimed as the "first 'Hamlet' ever seen in America". *Popping the Question*, a curtain raiser, and *Fazio* were on the bill for the second night. Fanny acted in both pieces and received a tremendous welcome, though Keppel, who was playing 'Fazio', did not know his lines. Mr. Hone was delighted with her rendering of 'Bianca', a part calculated for a display of the strongest passions of the female heart—love, hate, and jealousy. "I predicted before we went", he wrote in his diary, "that it would be no half-way affair; she would make the most decided hit we had ever witnessed or would fail entirely, and so it proved. I have never witnessed an audience so moved, astonished, and delighted. The curtain fell amid deafening shouts and plaudits. We have never seen her equal on the American stage."

Romeo and Juliet was next played by father and daughter, and then the *School for Scandal*, which did not seem to go well, for, though the house was full, people missed the jokes and sat stolidly quiet. As a matter of fact, comedy was not in Fanny's line and, though Charles Kemble made a very fine 'Charles Surface', she made a very poor 'Lady Teazle'. *Venice Preserved*, *Much Ado About Nothing*, *The Stranger*, and *The Hunchback*, were given in quick succession. New York playgoers decided, as London playgoers had already done, that 'Julia' was the part that suited Fanny best. Hone had never witnessed anything like her acting in this play: "She excels in the delineation of feeling highwrought and impassioned. . . ." "The house was full in every part, and never was an audience so moved and so delighted." *King John* and *The Inconstant* followed. David Wilkie, who happened to be in New York at the time, went to see "Kemble and his gifted daughter" act. He was fond of superlatives, and in his unpruned English wrote them down as "the Great Magic Stars of the Western World".

A few seasoned playgoers professed to detect in Fanny Kemble mannerisms, pomposity and a too deliberate bid for effect. Such critics were in a minority, however, and the writer in the *New York Mirror*, who could not trust mere words to convey his enthusiasm but expressed it by means of capital letters, accurately registered the emotional enjoyment of the great majority of Fanny's worshippers. "The great peculiarity of her acting is MIND. It is full of intellectual excellence. By this the audience as well as herself are carried away. She depicts tenderness, jealousy, hate, and despair with a truth that now melts the soul, now makes it tremble. . . . Her hate is sardonic, KEAN-LIKE, and almost intolerable; her love deeply impassioned and tender; all bashful girlishness and full of exquisitely graceful touches—FULL of them. Her fixed look of despair hushes every sound, till her silent glance of scorn shakes the house with sudden peals of thunder. This is indeed *acting*."

Considering how often *The Recruiting Officer* and *The Beaux' Stratagem* were given on the American stage, it was a surprise to Fanny to find that her audiences were shocked to think a young girl should play in anything so coarse as *The Inconstant*. She merely saw it as a drama which gave her father the opportunity of acting 'Mirabel' with consummate skill. After all, freedom of expression and manner were certainly not in her case an indication of laxity of morals. But how difficult it was for her to look at any of these plays from a detached, objective point of view, when they were so familiar! It was like asking a child to criticise the ethics of Red Riding Hood. Being a steady, conscientious impersonator, Fanny threw herself unquestioningly into her parts no matter what their character, and had no patience with artists who refused to identify themselves with vicious or ugly rôles and tried "to impress on an audience the wide difference between their assumed and real disposition by acting ill and looking as cross as they possibly could, which surely could not give satisfaction even to a highly moral audience". Fanny had often noticed interpreters of 'Aldabella' in *Fazio*, of the 'Queen' in *Hamlet*, of 'Margarita' in *Rule a Wife*, behaving in this way, whereas Aunt Sarah, her pattern, was "as true in her performance of the wretch 'Millwood' as in her personifications of Shakespeare's grandest creations".

The takings for the twelve performances at the Park Theatre were satisfactory, and the Kembles profited to the sum of seven hundred pounds. On concluding this engagement they crossed by steamship to the New Jersey shore, disembarked on an improvised jetty of rocks and planks, and mounted a stage "shaped like a boat, leathern sides buttoned down and with three seats to hold three persons each. This nefarious black hole is intended to carry nine; there is not really room for more than two good-sized people on a seat." It was the "wickedest road" over bog and marsh, and even

Charles Kemble's solid frame was jerked up to the roof every two or three minutes. There were fourteen coach loads of passengers, and they drove past untidy farms, broken gates and zigzag fences of poles or rails "like the herring-bone seam of a flannel petticoat". After a fourteen-mile drive the passengers got into a train drawn by horses along iron rails. The first carriage, into which Fanny jumped, had scarlet leather seats and woollen curtains to match. The train, in every way an improvement on the stage, moved smoothly and slowly towards the Delaware, where they found a "piggery" of a steamship which conveyed them to Philadelphia. The spitting was terrible, but then it was also terrible at rehearsals on the stage, and Fanny was to some extent broken in to the habit. It often happened that her white muslin dress, freshly laundered in the morning, had to be put into the wash-tub at night stained all over with tobacco juice. "Gentlemen spit on the carpets of rooms in which they are talking to ladies. Did you ever know such a country?" A quiet Scottish clergyman travelling at this time observed that the incessant spitting reminded him so much of rain that he had "an almost irresistible propensity to open an umbrella".

The Kembles took their boxes to the Mansion House —Mr. Head's hotel, and as usual Fanny went out to find a bath-house and was mildly surprised to find two baths in one room, but then, she writes, "the people of this country have an aversion for solitude". She is one of the few travellers of this date who ever mentions a bath-house. Others seem to have been content with the basins and wooden foot tubs they found in the hotels.

Their five-night engagement at the Chestnut Street Theatre opened with *Hamlet*. On the same night Edwin Forrest produced Bird's Peruvian tragedy *Oraloossa* at the Arch Street playhouse. Managers were apprehensive lest these two great attractions should prove mutually destructive. There were enough playgoers, however, in Philadelphia to fill both houses for five nights, so everyone was pleased. At *Fazio* Fanny found the audience "sticky" and "unapplauding". "It was horrid not to know whether one was giving satisfaction or not." For *Romeo and Juliet* the house was the most unsympathetic she had ever played to, "literally immovable". "They always wait to the end and then applaud or go away quietly." In order to do justice to 'Mrs. Beverly', whose raiment had been left in New York, Fanny ordered "a beautiful claret-coloured velvet which will cost Miss Kemble eleven guineas by this living light".

Mr. Wood of the Chestnut Street theatre, who acted with the Kembles in most of their plays, including the name parts in *Fazio* and *King John*, was delighted with their season, and records that "the receipts were uniformly great". The success of both Forrest and the Kembles was the more surprising when one remembers that they were playing to people whose minds were focussed on the forthcoming Presidential election. Nothing else was talked about. Very little was to be heard of Henry Clay, but mysterious arguments about

"Nullifiers" and "Old Hickory" caught Fanny's ears in the hotel, and from the window she heard cheering and "rabblement", and watched star-spangled banners and "villainous transparencies" of Jackson being carried about. It was remarkable that any good American could settle down for a quiet evening in Verona or Peru when such excitement was present in the streets.

Returning to New York after their week in Philadelphia, the Kembles played again at the Park Theatre. *The Hunchback* was performed four times: it had a prodigious success. Charles Kemble attended the Tammany Hall banquet to celebrate Jackson's election, and it was something of a surprise to both father and daughter to find that the 25th of November, the anniversary of the evacuation of the city by British troops, was still celebrated with patriotic devotion and thankfulness.

A benefit had been fixed for their old friend John Howard Payne, who had fallen on evil days. The Kembles were included in the galaxy of stars which performed in his honour, and a rather heavy programme, consisting of *Brutus*, *Charles II.*, and *Katharine and Petruchio*, was presented to a long-suffering audience. All seats save the gallery had been raised to five dollars. In the pit, normally reserved for men, sat ladies of fashion and officers in uniform. The receipts totalled seven thousand dollars, which was considered highly satisfactory by playwright and promoters.

Henry Clay saw and admired Fanny as 'Violante' in *The Wonder*, a part played with great success by her mother twenty years earlier. Clay noted that Kemble was what, in the polite parlance of the day, was called a little *"dans les vignes du Seigneur"*. This state of affairs always made Fanny nervous, and something, possibly her father's addiction to cocktails and gin slings, put her out of conceit with acting altogether. How despicable was mumming, how vile the mimicry of scenery! Pasteboard and paint for the thick breathing orange groves of the South; green silk and oiled parchment for the splendours of her moon at night; wooden platforms and canvas curtains for solid marble balconies! Pretence, pretence; how could acting be counted as an art when it created nothing! Aunt Sarah had once said, "My brother John in his most impetuous bursts is always careful to avoid any discomposure of dress or deportment, but in the whirlwind of passion I lose all thought of such matters". That was the measure of the difference between them as artists. Was it perhaps because she herself was no real artist, Fanny wondered, that on some nights in spite of all her efforts every word turned to burlesque?

Lying on the stage one night by a strange 'Romeo', she fumbled for the dagger and frightened a very incompetent actor by muttering, "Where the devil is your dagger?" After the performance she told her father that she really could not be a party to converting *Romeo and Juliet* into a farce again. Next morning a bouquet of shell flowers arrived at her hotel as an apology from an inadequate stage lover.

§ VIII

The Kembles' second expedition to Philadelphia in December was quieter and pleasanter than the first, because the election fever was over and people had time to take notice of them socially, though a faint prejudice against actors was observable in the more select circles. Flowers, candies, and a few cards arrived, and there was dancing and riding to be enjoyed, and dear Washington Irving's *Knickerbocker History of New York* to laugh over. Christmas Day was rather depressing. English people associate it with happy family parties. "Here", Fanny observed, "there is no home clinging; indeed, it is scarcely a holiday." They were billed to play *Macbeth*, for the theatres, to her surprise, were open. To one who felt that she resembled "the Great Mogul quite as much as Lady Macbeth" it was a trying effort. She only hoped that Aunt Sarah was not a witness to her performance.

They were informed by the manager of the theatre that Tyrone Power from England was due to arrive at the Front Street Theatre, but his plays appealed to a different class of audience, and there was no rivalry between them as in the case of a serious play like *Oraloossa*. Finding the Kembles already established in the city, Power "gave these attractive objects a wide berth", but, "I had the greater success", he says triumphantly, "as appealing to the pit".

Fanny and her father went on to Baltimore and put up at Barnum's Hotel for New Year to play at the

Holliday Street Theatre, a large, handsome, dirty, dilapidated place, "looking as if there had been eleven executions that morning". Visiting the Cathedral for benediction brought back school-days in France, but even here there was spitting, and by the priests too, on altar steps and carpet. Their short engagement fulfilled, the Kembles proceeded to Washington by "exclusive extra" along the usual bad bumping road. Fanny's description of what she saw from the windows of the post-chaise might have been written to-day: "The leaves of the black oak wither but do not fall, and give a stricken, blighted air to the landscape. . . . The stunted cedars, silver barked button-wood, red-yellow ravines and water-courses, give it a peculiar character."

They stayed at Gadsby's, "an inn like a little town with more wooden flights of steps, passages, doorways, exits and entrances than any town I ever saw; it reminded me of the house in Tieck's *Love Charm*". Such ridiculous things happened: they met a man who had "pagan-ed" his three sons, Romulus, Remus, and Tiberius, and she discovered that the waiter who handed her the bread was "pagan-ed" Horatius. Goodness! How she and Aunt Dall laughed over these things.

The theatre at Washington was the tiniest box of a place, "not much bigger than the baby's play-house at Versailles". "The stage, when one was on it, seemed but half a yard from the boxes." Philip Hone, after seeing Fanny performing there, said it made him think of "a canary in a mouse-trap". And yet two years earlier it had been enlarged to accommodate one thousand persons and, though small, was considered a most up-to-date theatre. There were three tiers of boxes, a new furnace heater, a coffee-room, and modern but untrustworthy gas illumination. On going down to rehearse, Fanny found the same excellent "old Drury" company she had acted with at Baltimore, and was able to go sightseeing with a clear conscience.

Justice Story of the Supreme Court, who watched her play Mrs. Haller in the *Stranger*, wrote to his wife: "The audience was moved to tears. The Chief Justice Marshall was present and shed them in common with younger eyes." So moved was Justice Story by Fanny's acting that he composed an ode in her praise.

> Genius and taste and feeling all combine
> To make each province of the drama thine.
> She first to Fanny's bright creation gives
> The very form and soul: it breathes, it lives.
> She next with grace inimitable plays
> In every gesture, action, tone, and gaze.
> The last to Nature lends its subtlest art
> And warms and thrills and melts the heart.
> Go, lovely woman, go! enjoy thy fame,
> A second Kemble with a deathless name.

Senators, Congressmen, and members of the Government all flocked to the little theatre. "Fanny Kemble is here turning everyone's head," wrote Daniel Webster. "I went to see and hear her last evening, and paid for it by a tremendous cold. I hear that the venerable judges go constantly." Between plays the Kembles squeezed in as many sights as possible, visiting the Capitol and staying for a while in the Senate Chamber. When they arrived, Webster was addressing two semi-circles of senators, and literally sitting among them— Fanny could hardly believe her eyes—were a whole regiment of ladies whispering, talking, laughing, and fidgeting. The gallery, which was on a level with the floor—a mere railed-off space, was also filled with pink, yellow, and blue bonnets. Every now and again there was a fresh rustle of silks and waving of feathers, and a new stream of political beauties would arrive, pushing their way through and how-d'ye-doing and shaking hands. Webster, who was talking in his sonorous voice about French raids on American commerce, appeared, in spite of his great power of concentration, to be bothered by so much frivolity. The heat in the small Senate Chamber was so intolerable that the Kembles fled away to the more spacious hall in which the Representatives deliberated. There they found members with feet on desks being addressed by speakers who to the Kembles were all inaudible. Of course, they visited the unpretentious White House, fenced from the highway by wooden palings. It looked to them un-cared for, with its surrounding of withered grass and its desolate reach of marshland stretching to the river. Of course, too, they shook hands with President Jackson, who talked about South Carolina and the Nullifiers, and protested against scribbling ladies, assuring Miss Kemble, with a smile, that all the trouble had originated "in the nib of the pen of a lady".

On winter mornings of bright sunshine Fanny rode
out with various cavaliers, but did not get on terms
with American steeds. According to her they "shambled
along at a rack" or "pulled like the devil" at the snaffle
bridle. Being accustomed to riding on a curb she complained feelingly of the want of manners in her mounts,
and was also unguarded enough to say that Americans
could not sit a horse properly, and that the left not the
right should be the rule of the road, all of which remarks
tended to make her unpopular with her cavaliers.

Sometimes she had to wend her way over the marshland and moorland "called the city" to return cards. It
seemed to her a preposterous town, ten miles square
at least, with houses dotted here and there in an untamed wilderness. She thought of the way her old friend
Tom Moore had poked fun at the place. The opening
lines of his *Epistle to Lord Forbes*, for example, had a
peculiar relish on the spot that inspired them:

> And what was Goose Creek once is Tiber now!
> This famed metropolis, where Fancy sees
> Squares in morasses, obelisks in trees;
> Which travelling fools and gazetteers adorn
> With shrines unbuilt and heroes yet unborn,
> Though nought but wood and . . . they see,
> Where streets should run, and sages *ought* to be!

Americans have always had faith in the imaginations
of their hearts, a faith justified by stupendous achievement, but, to Tom Moore, Fanny Kemble, and other
English people brought up to distrust rapid growth as
something in itself unsound, it has always been a

matter of suspicion when objects expand and events move at a different rate from that to which they are accustomed at home.

Fanny, like many of her compatriots, was disposed to laugh at American ways. Coming back to the hotel after an excursion on horseback, she found a man talking earnestly to her father. "Fanny," said Charles Kemble, "pray, can you call to mind anything you said during the course of your Thursday's ride which was likely to be offensive to Mr. —— or anything abusive of this country?" Rather nettled, she untied her bonnet quietly and then said, "I do not now recollect a word I said during my whole ride, and shall certainly not give myself the trouble to do so". "Now, my dear," said her father, "don't put yourself into a passion, compose yourself and recollect." He then read a letter aloud accusing her of having spoken in a manner derogatory to America and the Americans, and threatening that unless she apologized she would be hissed off the stage. Harassed, Charles Kemble added that over fifty members of Congress had already mentioned the matter to him. What was he to do about it? "Deny it, of course," said Fanny, feeling very angry and rather guilty at having let her tongue run away with her. In an entry in her diary to the effect that "another so unhappily sensitive a community surely never existed in the world", she vainly tried to put the blame for her own bad manners on the Americans. "I would not advise Mrs. Trollope, Captain Basil Hall, or Major Thomas Hamilton ever to set their feet upon this ground again unless they are ambitious of being stoned to death. . . . I myself live in daily expectation of martyrdom."

The story pursued her, and when they played at Philadelphia for a third short season at the end of January, handbills reporting her conversation were thrown into the pit at the Walnut Street Theatre before the performance of *Fazio*. The text was as follows:

"FANNY KEMBLE—A letter from Washington of the 20th instant received in this city from a gentleman of undoubted veracity contains the following: Miss Fanny Kemble was introduced by one of her own countrymen to a gentleman of respectability and with whom she subsequently rode out on horseback. She observed in course of conversation with him that she had not seen a lady or gentleman fit for her to associate with since she came to America. When near home he (the gentleman with whom she had been conversing and whom she supposed to be an Englishman) told her he had the honour of being an American and that her sex alone protected her from a proper resentment of the insult given. What a comment on the fashionables of Philadelphia! Will they continue to pamper the heiress of Mrs. Trollope? Such conduct as this, coming from one who has had the praises and the purses of the American people lavished upon her without measure, ought to be particularly remembered, especially at her benefit."

A Philadelphia paper reported that Mr. Kemble had advanced to the front of the stage, and, after reading the handbill aloud with "great perspicuity" and firmness of manner, declared its contents wholly false. He added that the individual who so signalized his valour by insulting a female would have found in her father a protector ready to answer for anything she had done; moreover, since his daughter and himself had received the utmost kindness and attention in every city in America which they had visited: "if they could have used any such expressions they would have been amongst the most ungrateful people in the world". This address was loudly applauded. Fanny meanwhile sat shivering in the green-room, wishing she were "a caterpillar under a green gooseberry bush". An ovation, however, greeted her when she crept on to the stage crying bitterly.

The theatre was packed for the rest of the engagement, especially for Fanny's benefit; it was said the handbill had been so good an advertisement that Charles Kemble must have made it up himself. The stage-door was mobbed nightly, flowers and candies appeared in ever greater profusion, the advance booking was phenomenal, for the warm heart and chivalrous feeling of America had been roused by the sight of a frightened girl sobbing behind the footlights.

No American took a greater personal interest in Fanny Kemble than Thomas Sully, the Philadelphian portrait painter. He made a sketch of her head on his thumb-nail the first time he saw her act, and later executed studies of her as 'Julia', 'Lady Macbeth', 'Juliet', and 'Beatrice'. As Charles Kemble commissioned him to make a kit-cat likeness of him as 'Fazio' and one of

Fanny as 'Bianca', many hours were spent in his studio. It was there that Charles Kemble met John Sartain, the well-known engraver, and commissioned him to re-engrave his portrait as 'Secretary Cromwell' from Harlow's picture of the Kemble family playing in *Henry VIII*. When Sartain went to Head's Hotel in Spruce Street to deliver the proofs from the plate, he played a little joke upon "Miss Fanny". "I had previously engraved a portrait of Sir Thomas Lawrence after the fine print by Cousins, and I purposely placed the Lawrence on top so that it should be the first seen when opened. Miss Fanny was standing on the hearth with her back to the fire and her hands behind her. As the package was opened she naturally expected to see the portrait of her father, but to her astonishment there was that of her friend, Sir Thomas. The way in which her surprise and pleasure were expressed was worth witnessing. I expressly planned the surprise, and it was a success."

The Kembles were made a great deal of during this, their third visit to Philadelphia. Since Washington had accepted them they became quite the fashion. Exclusive Mrs. Caton, daughter of the grand old man of the city, Mr. Carroll, invited them to her house. Having three daughters married to Englishmen—Lady Wellesley, the Duchess of Leeds, and Lady Stafford—she was disposed to be interested in English visitors. Among other acquaintances were Dr. Mease and his son, Pierce Butler, who was already strongly attracted by Miss Kemble. They walked and rode by Wissahicon and found it beautiful. "I love Philadelphia for ever-more," wrote Fanny in her diary, and one suspects the reason for this confession was that she too had lost her heart. Edgar Allan Poe, a few years later, said: "It was not till Fanny Kemble in her droll book about the United States pointed out to Philadelphians the rare loveliness of a stream which lay at their own doors that this loveliness was more than suspected by a few adventurous pedestrians of the vicinity. But the *Journal* having opened all eyes, the Wissahicon rolled at once into notoriety."

§ IX

Returning to New York, Fanny played 'Lady Macbeth' for her own benefit on the 11th of February. The locally supplied witches turned out to be men, who played the parts as three jolly old fishwives in a manner as unlike as could be to the unearthly appearances described by 'Banquo'. During a short engagement *The Hunchback* was given twice, *The Merchant of Venice* once, and *The Wonder* was acted for the second time. On the 19th of February Miss Kemble's own play, *Francis I.*, was presented to an excited, expectant house. It was very well received, and repeated by request on the following night. At a benefit arranged for William Dunlap two days later, the Kembles appeared with Edwin Forrest in *Venice Preserved*, and Dunlap's own farce, *Bonaparte in England*, was included in the programme. Miss Catharine Sedgwick from Massa-

chusetts and her brother Robert, who lived in New
York, were entranced by Miss Kemble's presentation of
'Belvidera'. "I have never seen any woman on the stage
to be compared with her," wrote Miss Catharine to
Mrs. Channing in Boston. "She is a most captivating
creature steeped to the very lips in genius. . . . On the
stage she is beautiful, far more than beautiful, her face
is the mirror of her soul. . . . I have been to see her, she
is a quiet gentlewoman in her deportment." Having
seen *Francis I.*, Miss Catharine wrote ecstatically to
another friend that Fanny had given back to her something of the enraptured feeling of youth; and she had
"experienced from the mastery of genius" that "inde-
finable something that restores flexibility and fires and
melts you".

A friendship grew up between Fanny Kemble and
the Sedgwicks. Though Miss Catharine perhaps admired her most, it was to her niece, Elizabeth, that her
love went out, and later she became the recipient of
many confidences. It was in Miss Catharine's cheerful
home at Stockbridge, where all the crickets were supposed to chirp Sedgwick! Sedgwick! that refuge from
disillusionment was sought.

From New York the Kembles travelled to Boston
and opened at the Tremont Theatre with *Hamlet,*
followed on the next night by *Fazio.* The audience was
cold but attentive. Fanny was disposed to be a little
nervous, knowing how critical Bostonians were reputed
to be. One of her windows at the Tremont Hotel
looked out on to the box-office and the other on to the

graveyard in which stood the cenotaph erected by
Benjamin Franklin to his father. Which was the better
omen? For must not the one signify a full house and
the other the funeral of hopes? Fanny was not left long
in doubt, for, quite suddenly and unexpectedly, Boston
opened its arms to the Kembles. For *The Stranger*, an
old favourite, the house was sold out. Speculators
smeared in molasses (to avoid being pushed) bought all
the boxes and re-sold them at a profit. Fanny's spirits
rose despite her father's lameness and ill-temper, for
the stage-manager reported that "crowded houses
composed of the beauty and wealth of the city were
assembling to do honour to Miss Kemble and her
father".

The School for Scandal went down admirably, and so
did the rest of the repertory. Colonel Henry Lee, at that
time a lad, has left it on record that "no one who witnessed Miss Kemble's impersonations of 'Mrs. Beverly',
'Belvidera', 'Bianca', 'Julia', 'Portia', 'Katharine',
'Ophelia', 'Juliet', has ever had her image effaced from
his mind or has ever enjoyed a glimpse of her successor.
... The glamour of her apparition has not yet vanished.
... It seems but yesterday that we were all youths and
maidens, hanging round Tremont Place to see her
mount Niagara—a horse I rode thenceforth on holidays
and in vacations because she had been upon his back—
or scouring the country to have a glimpse of her as she
galloped past. Every young girl who could sported
Fanny Kemble curls. Flowers were hung on her door-
knob at the hotel, and Harvard students went crazy

about her. As long as funds held out they trooped across the river to Boston of an evening and waited in the narrow entrance alley like sardines in a tin and were borne along when the doors opened into the pit to sit absorbed on backless benches. Fanny played 'Bianca', and the young people went out transfixed with horror and fascination into uttermost darkness, and counted the hours and the cash that would bring them back. I remember one night when, as 'Belvidera', shrieking, stares at her husband's ghost, I was sitting in front, in her line of vision, and I cowered and shrank from her terrible gaze. How we all wept with her as 'Mrs. Beverly' over the frenzied despair of her gamester husband!— with this difference, that her tears were staining her silk dress while ours were mopped by our handker-chiefs. How we all enjoyed her shrewish outbursts and humble penitence as 'Katharine', and her father's assumed violence and real good breeding as 'Petruchio'. . . . Who has played 'Portia' with such sweet dignity? Who has so filled out the part of the whole-hearted 'Beatrice'?"

Staid young Bostonians were enthusiastic, cheered her every appearance and crowned her with roses. Young men, heedless of what had happened in Washington, took her out riding in the mornings, past "the beautiful little mere Jamaica Pond" and "the pretty village of Roxbury", where she secured a nosegay "for my Lady Teazle", and sometimes farther afield, though her boast to Mr. Adams of riding thirty miles a day before acting was excessive.

A few sights were visited; Chantrey's statue of Washington she had seen in his Pimlico studio, it now stood in the State House; Bunker Hill, as the place where so much English blood was shed, awoke sentiment and reflections, "for, after all, 'twas all English blood, and the fathers of the Yankees had trod the soil whereon has grown more goodness, more greatness, more beauty, more truth than on any other earth under God's sun".

A certain amount of unpleasantness was associated with the engagement in Boston. Charles Kemble had agreed with Mr. Dana, lessee of the Tremont Theatre, to play on the same terms as he had performed at the Park Theatre, New York, which he stated at the time he made the contract to be "half the houses", that is to say, one half the gross receipts. Under this arrangement the Kembles came to Boston. Some indignation was caused by his demand that the Federal Street Theatre should not remain open against him, and further bad opinions were formed later when it was discovered that he had not received "half the houses" at the Park Theatre but half the receipts after deducting $222 a night. In an action brought by Mr. Dana against Mr. Kemble months afterwards for recovery of the difference, the plaintiff was awarded the sum of $2220 by order of the Supreme Court of Massachusetts.

Though making a pleasant and dignified impression on the people he met in America, Charles Kemble was known by managers to be a hard man to deal with. A Boston newspaper, alluding to his "avarice" and other "ungentlemanly characteristics", congratulated Fanny when she married on escaping from his care. It was said in London that he had cleared fifteen thousand pounds by his American tour, and later his profits were estimated at twenty thousand pounds. Fanny's share of takings was limited to her benefits. At the end of her tour they were said to amount to six thousand pounds.

Among the homes in which the Kembles were entertained in Boston was that of Dr. George Parkman, who later was murdered by Professor Webster. At this house Fanny met John Quincy Adams, whose comments on Shakespeare gave her something to reflect over. She tells us that the ex-President, while sitting next to her at dinner, mildly remarked that *The Hunchback* was by no means so good as Shakespeare. "Shakespeares do not grow on every bush," retorted Fanny. He replied: "I am a worshipper of Shakespeare but find *Othello* disgusting, *Lear* ludicrous, and *Romeo and Juliet* childish nonsense". Fanny slowly drank a tumbler of water in order to concoct a reply, but, finding nothing suitable to say, changed the conversation and told him of her prowess as a horsewoman. On returning home Mr. Adams made an entry in his diary to the effect that he had had a conversation with Miss Kemble "chiefly upon dramatic literature, but that it differed not from what it might have been with any intelligent and well-educated young woman of her age". But, as all readers of his memoirs know, he was not easily impressed, and, as all readers of Fanny Kemble's diaries know, she was apt to dramatize conversations and experiences.

Many Bostonians showed the Kembles hospitality. Dr. Channing, the famous Unitarian preacher, was especially civil. He gave Fanny one of Miss Martineau's tales—*Ella of Garveloch*—to amuse her, with the warning that the author had not sufficient grasp of the principles of political economy to make useful her works on that subject. Miss Catharine Sedgwick presented "the poet-actress" with a copy of her novel, *Hope Leslie*, and confirmed by further intercourse her delighted first impressions of Fanny's genius and charm.

Eclipsing all those reasonable associations was a passionate courtship, that of Pierce Butler of Philadelphia. He had pursued Fanny to Boston, and, from sheer devotion, played the flute in the orchestra at her benefit. This young man, of good family, good looks, and great personal charm, was "incessant", as the newspaper had it, "in his attentions to her". They galloped over Nahant sands together and dismounting played with seaweeds and shells; they talked of love in Mount Auburn cemetery, then a rural park with scarce a grave in it. When the Kembles left Boston to play in Albany, Pierce Butler accompanied them, but it was not till October 1833 that Mr. Stephen Price on arriving in London from New York told his friends that Miss Kemble was engaged to be married, but that her stage contracts must be fulfilled till June 1834.

At the end of September the Kembles returned from a Canadian holiday to New York in order to resume work. They opened with *The Stranger* and then produced *The Wife*, a new play by Sheridan Knowles, which was so well received that they had to repeat it five times.

Soon after her engagement was made public Fanny met Washington Irving. He greeted her warmly, but took the opportunity of giving her good advice. "So I hear you are going to be married and settle in this country. Well, you will be told this country is like your own and that living in it is like living in England, but do not believe it. It is no such thing, nothing of the sort, which need not prevent you being very happy here if you make the best of things as you find them. Above all, whatever you do don't become a creaking door. . . ." "What's that?" asked Fanny. He told her his friend, Leslie, had married an Englishwoman and brought her out to America, but she worried and tormented his and her own life out with ceaseless complaints and comparisons, and was such a nuisance that he "used to call her the creaking door". Miss Catharine Sedgwick was none too happy about the engagement. Though she thought Pierce Butler "a gentlemanly man, with good sense, and amiable disposition, he was 'so infinitely inferior' to Fanny that the experiment of marriage must be dangerous". She records her "thousand fears of the result".

Chit Chat and other London society papers often contained paragraphs about Fanny. At this time she was said to be engaged to a man of great wealth and of the highest respectability. Sometimes he was described as a Butler of Ormonde, sometimes as a person who had assumed the name of Butler in order to inherit a property, sometimes as the youngest of seven sons. In another paper he figured as "a fine young man" with "a fortune of £4000 a year" and "more to come from two rich aunts". Hope was expressed in one periodical that the marriage might take place in England, while another announced that Mrs. Kemble and family were leaving immediately for America in order to be present at the wedding in Philadelphia. Social paragraphs have not changed much in character in a hundred years.

§ x

Whatever was true or untrue about Pierce Butler it is certain that he and Fanny were passionately in love with each other, and that for him she considered her career well lost. The tempestuous infatuation submerged all considerations of country, family, pride in her profession and independence. Reporters noted that she looked thinner and less pleasing since she had become engaged, but then they did not know how deeply Fanny had felt the tragedy of Aunt Dall's death from a carriage accident. Mummers cannot mourn openly, and on the very day of her aunt's funeral she had been obliged to fulfil a theatrical engagement.

After playing in New York in December 1833, the Kembles acted again in Baltimore and Washington, and then repeated all their former successes at a further engagement in New York, beginning on April 24, 1834, adding to the plays already presented, *Rule a Wife and Have a Wife*, *Henry VIII.*, and *Charles II*. At the termination of this little season Fanny made preparations for her wedding, and by the 6th of June *The Star-Spangled Banner*, a Philadelphia paper, was able to announce that the Right Reverend Bishop White had united "Pierce Butler, Esq., of this city to Miss Frances Anne Kemble of England" in the bonds of wedlock.

After an ecstatic five weeks' honeymoon Fanny acted again in New York. She opened with 'Bianca', and then in rapid sequence played in *The Honeymoon, Romeo and Juliet, The School for Scandal, The Wife, Katharine and Petruchio, Venice Preserved, Jane Shore* (her aunt's great part taken for the first time), *The Hunchback*, and *The Stranger*.

With characteristic generosity Fanny made over the £6000 she had earned in America as a parting gift to her father, who sailed for England on the 24th of June. Miss Sedgwick records that Fanny was under an engagement to perform another year for her father should he require her, but "as he went off in a pet with Butler, his pride may save her that misery".

§ XI

To begin with, Fanny and her husband were extremely happy. For his sake she began to learn book-keeping, and wrote to Miss Sedgwick: "Now pray exclaim aloud as I have done internally a thousand times since I began to learn this most matter-of-fact of sciences 'great is the power of love'!" Her new home, "Butler Place", or, as she tactlessly called it, "The Farm", was situated six miles from Philadelphia.

It was a small country house built in 1790 by a French architect, and, being of a design unusual in Pennsylvania, was very much admired by the neighbours. The façade consisted of two superimposed columned "galleries" on to which the rooms opened. Mansard windows revealed French influence, as did the terrace in front of the house—a low brick wall on which stood a row of orange-trees in tubs. The air of formality given by the shrubs and the line of the wall were in themselves attractive in a country in which the surroundings of human habitations are often rough and unkempt. Large locust trees stood round about, and the white dwelling-house, with its orangery at the rear, its three acres of vegetable garden, and three hundred acres of woodland and grass, formed a most charming little country place of the type that in England would be designated as Manor.

Fanny likened the place to "a second-class farm in England, though in America", and the inference is obvious, "it passed for a model country mansion". When asked by curious visitors how the place compared with the majority of country seats in her own land, she gave a good deal of offence by saying that to her it appeared farm-like and hardly an abode for gentlefolk. There must have been some reason for her to disparage the place in this way; possibly it was her reaction to the American habit of "puffery", possibly it was caused by resentment at finding that her husband's family did not show due appreciation of her importance. Perhaps some of her new relations did not think that Pierce had done too well for himself in marrying an actress, and that Fanny retorted by sniffing at the chief object of their pride. Probably, too, she talked of the great country houses in which she had stayed in England, but, of course, that did not deceive her American acquaintances, for they knew perfectly well that she was accustomed to a player's life and had never had anything half so nice as Butler Place to call her own. Something in her new life disappointed her terribly. It may quite easily have been that she missed the approbation of the public and the variety in love-making incidental to acting, but, whatever the reason, life at Butler Place was tedious beyond belief once the first romantic glamour had worn off the experience of matrimony. Feverishly, Fanny set to work to make flower-beds in front of the terrace and an English lawn. She also rearranged the rooms in a way more reminiscent of home.

In letters to England she complained that no neighbours welcomed her arrival, as would have been the case at home, and that the poorer country people appeared oddly suspicious of her advances. What could she find to do planted down six miles from a city? The road was impossibly bad for driving, and Pierce rode in every day to work in an office in Philadelphia. As she had six servants, there was nothing in the way of household duties with which she could occupy herself; her day was completely free and also completely solitary.

At first she brushed up her Latin and then began to

prepare her *Journal* for the press. Writing to a friend
in England on the subject of this diary, she observes,
"No book has a chance of succeeding in the United
States unless the Americans are abused in it". Miss
Sedgwick, to whom she confided her project, replied
by confessing to "flutterings" of nervousness. Fanny
scolded her, and said that every sheet as it went to
press would be submitted to the soberer judgement
of her husband with his 'American ear' and 'American
eye' for what might offend.

In the autumn, Harriet Martineau arrived in Philadelphia to stay with Dr. and Mrs. Furness. Fanny was
considerably awed by her reputation and manner, but,
after a short acquaintance, summoned up courage to
submit the proof-sheets of her book to the great
authoress. Curiosity makes one wonder by what passages the reader was sufficiently shocked to persuade her
young friend to suppress thirty pages of print. Fanny
was eager, insensitive, and confiding. Little did she
guess when she deferred to the judgement of this
paragon spinster how fundamentally Harriet Martineau
shrank from intimacy with so passionate a young
woman. It was vain to try and analyse such repugnance.
What could it spring from? Harriet asked herself. Was
it that there was something incurably vulgar about
passion, or was it that these Kembles all had the green-
room cast of mind?

May 1835 saw the birth of Fanny's first child and the
publication of her *Journal*. The curtain that is drawn
over these early years of marriage is only pulled aside

by the one English visitor. When Harriet Martineau appeared again in Philadelphia, she graced the christening of Fanny's little daughter with her presence. Further efforts were made by her not to be narrow or stiff in judgement; she really strove hard to like and approve Fanny, but it was all in vain. "I imposed upon myself for a time as on others in conversation the belief that I did so; but I could not carry it on long. There was so radical an unreality about her and her sayings and doings, and so perverse a sporting with her possessions and privileges in life and with other people's peace, that my interest in her died out completely in a way which could not have happened if I could have believed her notorious fortunes to have been other than self-inflicted. By her way of entering upon marriage, and her conduct in it afterwards she deprived herself of all title to wonder at or complain of her domestic miseries, terrible as they were. She was a finely gifted creature wasted and tortured by want of discipline, principle, and self-knowledge." So much for a spinster view of Fanny Butler. It was severe and condemnatory in a superior style, but even Miss Martineau had to admit the existence of "terrible miseries". What they were we do not know, but they eventually resulted in a complete rupture with her husband.

§ XII

Since Fanny's chief object in publishing her *Journal* was to make a little money, she determined that the book had to be bright and caustic; but how difficult it was to know just what to leave out! Asterisks played the part of tombstones for some thoughts, and dashes served to throw a cloak of anonymity over people alluded to; but she seems to have overlooked the fact that Mr. Hone and Judge Story, for example, to say nothing of other people, could easily substitute letters for asterisks and names for dashes. Mr. Hone could read a contemptuous account of the dinner he gave to welcome them in New York. It was "tolerably well-dressed but ill-served", and "there were neither water-glasses nor finger-glasses". "The women were in a sort of French demi-toilette with bare necks and long sleeves, heads frizzled out after the very last petit-courier, and thread net handkerchiefs and capes, the whole of which appeared a strange marrying of incongruities. After dinner we had coffee but no tea, whereat my English stomach was in high dudgeon. . . . I was not a little amused at Mrs. —— asking me whether I had heard of Mr.—— singing or their musical soirées, and seeming all but surprised that I had no revelation of either across the Atlantic." Impertinent little comments on hospitality kindly tendered, but not more impertinent than her allusion to Justice Story. "Judge —— the most exquisite original I have met with even in this land of abundance!" His conversation was "interrupted every two minutes by a dexterous, expectoral interjection, which caused me nearly to jump off my chair in dismay". The publication of the book was a tactless business on the part of a bride newly settled in her husband's country, and did not serve to draw sympathy to Fanny when misfortune overtook her. On the whole, Edgar Allan Poe was right in saying that her taste left something to be desired. In reviewing the *Journal* for the *Southern Literary Messenger*, he wrote of it not so much as a foreign libel on America, but as a badly written book full of vulgarities. He objected to words like "dawdled", "gulped", "pottering", "grumpily", "doldrumish", and quotes the phrase, "When the gentlemen joined us they were all more or less 'how com'd you so indeed'," to illustrate her coarseness. "For a female to speak thus confidently", he says, "is indelicate." After all, Fanny and her critic were living in the days when "legs" were "limbs"!

Other writers accused her of being censorious and supercilious about the manners and institutions of her adopted country. Mrs. Charles Kemble, reading it in England, threw it on the ground several times: it amused and disgusted her by turns. Charles Kemble told Charles Greville that he had never read the book till it appeared in print, and that it was full of "sublime things and vulgarities".

§ XIII

In 1836 a change of fortune came to Fanny and her husband. Through the death of an aunt, Pierce and his brother John inherited a property which included a plantation in Georgia. None of the younger members of the family knew much about this place. It had been acquired before the Revolution by their grandfather, Major Pierce Butler, but since his death it had ceased to be a residential estate, and had been conducted as a business enterprise by a manager who had remitted money regularly to his employers. The young men were naturally curious about their new possession and arranged to winter at Butler's Island and explore its possibilities. The new situation created by the bequest was seized by Fanny as a golden opportunity to visit England. "Fanny Butler", wrote Miss Sedgwick, "is leading a quiet domestic life, idolizing her sweet baby and preparing for her visit home. I fear it will be hard work for her to come back again." Fanny sailed for England with the baby and Margery, the nurse, only too delighted at the chance of getting back to familiar scenes after two experimental years in Pennsylvania. Like all people who marry out of their own nation she had taken on something alien, and England was no longer the same, because she no longer was completely English. It was an intense joy for her to see her family and her friends, but, somehow, things were different; she had dropped out, she was no longer the popular actress, but a person who had as it were committed suicide and now had come back as an Americanized ghost.

Returning sadly to Butler Farm, feeling that she was a denizen neither of heaven nor hell, she bore another child, and sought occasional distraction in the society of the Sedgwicks at Stockbridge. Though Fanny loved her children and was a good mother, her marriage was a cankering disappointment. Pierce Butler, whom she never describes and rarely mentions, is known to us only by reflection in the minds of others. It would appear from his flute-playing, his bound volumes of French and Italian music, and the charming memories that he left behind him, that he was a cultivated, courteous Southern gentleman, but perhaps, being a young man of temperament and susceptibility, accustomed to female adoration, his bickerings with Fanny and their radically different outlook on life caused his passion for her to fade, as fade it did, and since the marriage was not based on mutual understanding, nothing agreeable or lasting in the way of comradeship took its place. Gossip in London soon reported him to be almost coldly indifferent to his wife and wearied by her excitability. The truth was that success had come too easily to Fanny. There had never been any proving of her metal. Life at the theatre had run smoothly as in a groove. You learnt your parts, you acted them, you received the applause that was your due, you were then suitably entertained; there was no responsibility attaching to such a life. Then she became the wife of an American husband and had to stand on her own feet, and express the woman she essentially was in her life and words, without being able to take refuge from troubles in the assumed characters of 'Bianca' or' Juliet' or 'Violante', and she did not like it. Though living was so far more difficult than acting, there was no applause to be won, and the absence of it was part of the unendurable tedium of existence at Butler Place.

Practically everything in America was uncongenial.

During the early, delirious months of marriage she was gay and happy, and rejoicing in her release from the stage. Her husband was ardent, devoted, musical; all that a lover should be. Perhaps it was the editing of her own diary, possibly the attitude of neighbours; but whatever the secret cause she slowly became critical and difficult to please. The sense of superiority that seems to be evoked in many English people by American intercourse took with her an aggressive turn which did not make for domestic peace.

The baby girls took up a good deal of her time and thoughts. Margery, the nurse she had engaged to look after them, was devoted as nurses only know how to be; but her beneficent reign was cut short a few years later when Fanny discovered that her eldest daughter was beginning to lisp the Rosary, which only shows how far Roger Kemble's grandchild had departed from the old Catholic, family tradition.

The Butler babies had illnesses like other children; like other mothers she worried over them. In these days of rapid tonsilectomy it is not without interest to look back on the methods of a century ago, as practised on Fanny's elder child. A small double-barrelled silver tube with a wire passed through it to form a loop or noose at one end; the wire was slipped over the tonsil, tightened at the neck, left in the mouth for twenty-four hours, and then removed. The tonsil was left to "rot off", a nauseous business both for patient and nurse.

In the summer of 1838 it was decided that the whole

family should move to Georgia for the winter. The
prospect was delightful to every member of the little
household. Fanny was thrilled at the prospect of seeing
slavery at first hand. New England friends wrote
begging her not to go in a prejudiced frame of mind,
and she replied: "Assuredly I *am* going prejudiced
against slavery, for I am an English woman in whom
the absence of such a prejudice would be disgraceful."

When arrangements were complete, the family party,
consisting of Mr. and Mrs. Pierce Butler, two baby
girls, and Margery, the nurse, took ship at Baltimore.
As they steamed down Chesapeake Bay Fanny had her
nose in *Oliver Twist*, a new and thrilling book, and
long enough to last several days. At Portsmouth
(Virginia) they landed, and took the stage which
carried them through a vast swamp punctuated with
dark cypress trees, black pools, and giant creepers.
At Weldon they got out to take the train. After
struggling in a dirty shack with tough ham and
half-baked bread, they mounted up into high little
railway carriages, only to be bundled out at sundown
into a stage-coach to splash over a corduroy road
through the long night. Daybreak found them at
Stantonsburg at another shack; no towel or glass
obtainable; eggs handed them begrimed with smoke
and powdered with cinders; milk full of dust and dirt.
It was well enough for the baby, whom Fanny was
nursing, but Margery was hard put to it to get food
suitable for the elder child. At Waynesborough, another
halting-place, they met an apparently hospitable colonel,

"a fellow fighter with Washington", living in a wood cabin. He sheltered ten of the travellers and charged them fifty cents each to their surprise, for they had imagined themselves guests. From here a train took them to Wilmington. Thence a steamer carried them to Charleston, another steamer to Savannah, and yet another to Darien. Travelling at this time was more tiresome than it had ever been, because of changes from stage to rail and the consequent delays.

At Darien they entered their kingdom; two boats manned by slaves met them, and they rowed off magnificently in one, leaving the luggage to follow in the second. This entry of the feudal lords amongst their dusky vassals was beginning to be very exciting, and Fanny's eyes darted about in observation as the boat swung along General Oglethorpe's canal to the Altamaha, a vast river with four branches, each bigger than the Thames. As they approached "Butler's Island" the steersman took up a huge conch and heralded their approach with strange, melancholy blasts. Negroes swarmed on the landing-stage chattering with excitement. Fanny found her hands and clothes kissed, her velvet pelisse stroked, her babies worshipped. It was as if great white gods had condescended to visit the regions of Erebus.

"Butler's Island" formed part of the family estate. It was eight miles round and contained some thousands of acres, mainly given to the cultivation of rice. The living house was built of boards. Looking out from it one saw an expanse of turbid water lapping against low banks of land and vibrating sedges. Behind the island lay the town of Darien, with its white, gable-ended warehouses, little churches, and hooting steamers. The house, built for a manager, had two fair-sized rooms on the ground floor, one used as bedroom, one as sitting-room, and three small rooms off them, one used as dressing-room, one as office, and one as the manager's bedroom. The attic above was given over to Margery and the babies. A detached kitchen stood to one side of the residence and an outhouse. That was all there was to know about the building, which was as plain as any building could be. The partitions were of wood, the main walls plastered within and whitewashed. The furniture was austere and home-made, wash-stands, clothes-press, sofas, tables were of pine wood, planed to the smoothness of satin. There were wooden latches to all doors, and caps, keys, coats hung from nails on the partitions. Cedar tubs, made on the place, served as baths. During the day the steam rice mill hummed its monotonous song close to the house. Opposite the mill stood the cook's shop, where the daily ration of rice and corn grits was boiled and distributed by an old woman to the slaves. Near by was the cooper's shop, where tubs, buckets, and rice barrels were put together, and the blacksmith's shop where iron articles for household or farm use were made. Three other villages, or, as the negroes called them, "camps", were situated on the island.

Round the back of the dwelling-house ran a ditch three feet wide, emptied and filled twice a day by the tide. It bounded the backyard like a moat, and its far bank consisted of a steep dyke with a few weeping willows growing on it. The whole island, at high tide, was lower than the waters about it. As Fanny walked exploringly along these dykes, "her only promenade", she had the river on one side, the tall rattling sedges on the other, while beyond lay the forest of stagnant pools, wild myrtle, giant magnolias, and spiked palmetto, and then the rice-fields mapped out in squares. Duck, snipe, geese, and turkeys, she put them all up in her wanderings, and longed for a shotgun. Overhead swung the great turkey-buzzards in the blue dome, mocking birds sang as they balanced on creepers that festooned the trees, and in front of her, across the path, darted birds like winged flames.

To give an outlet for some of her youthful spirits she took to rowing with "Jack", a young slave, for attendant. Days were spent fishing for that "heavenly fish", the white mullet of the Altamaha, and for shad, which were also excellent to eat. Lessons learned at Weybridge were put to use, but nothing ever took the bait save perch and cat-fish. However, it was enchanting to be in the open air. "I am only half a soul. I am so bound up with outward things, flowers and trees and scenes", wrote Fanny revelling in her new freedom. Her "darling little canoe", *Dolphin*, named after the rollicking porpoises that tore up the river in pursuit of the shad and mullet she could never hook, was paddled out in the saffron brightness of mornings, in the blue brilliance of noon or in the rosy softness of sunset.

"Claude Lorraine and Italy may go hang themselves together"; nothing could compare with the lovely variations of sky and atmosphere in Georgia. Sitting in her canoe by stone steps she watched girls with cedar piggins fetching water and bearing it away on their heads. Could one but see life here always, always as a series of pictures, romantic, exotic, strange, and not as the economic foundation of personal life, all would be beautiful beyond compare. Dreamlike and visionary, the coloured clouds appeared above the sun's rising and setting; great barges piled with cotton floated lazily from the upper river reaches to Darien; the one-toned horn sounded in the quiet twilight; slaves sang chanties in the darkness, and, to crown all, there were the scents of the magnolia, the orange, and jasmine flowers. An ineffable quality permeated the radiant mornings and still evenings by the dykes of Altamaha.

But the vision faded as the facts of life obtruded themselves upon Fanny's consciousness. There was the household, for example, looking to her for orders. It was composed of a man cook, a dairy woman, a laundry woman, the housemaid her daughter, and two young footmen. So many coloured people to wait on a little white family in a six-roomed house! What could they all do, and where did they all sleep? Not in bedrooms, that was self-evident, but, when work was over, they retired to hovels or the kitchen hearth. They seemed to her entirely unconsidered, for no time was set apart for their meals; they ate when they were hungry, squatting on their hams round the cook's fire. Fanny made inquiries, and was told that the boys slept on the ground and the women on rough board bedsteads softened by grey moss. To her inexperienced nostrils the household servants smelt horribly and appeared to be encrusted with dirt. It was difficult to tolerate waiters who made their presence obvious in this way. . . . Washing and clean linen were the first things to insist on, for the smell, Fanny felt, might be eliminated by the judicious use of soap and water, though the manager put it forward as a reason why slaves they must remain.

To the hordes of fowls in the piazza and garden she attributed the fleas and other vermin with which they began to be pestered. When one came to look into things on the estate neither men nor animals seemed to be well cared for. Lanky pigs appeared and miserable looking cows and sheep nosed about near the house seeking herbage. They were kept alive on rice flour and were occasionally sent by barge to St. Simon's Island to graze there.

It was all rather disconcerting, for, however keen a reformer one might be, it was difficult to know where to begin improving things, and there was no one to talk the problems over with, for the question of reforms did not interest Pierce. There was much to observe about this strange life; she was for ever making notes as the days passed rhythmically by. On Saturdays the negroes usually put off in boats to sell their poultry, eggs, and moss in shops at Darien. On one Sunday in the month they were allowed to go over to church there to a special Baptist Slave Church with a white minister who was himself a slave owner. Fanny wrote to Elizabeth Sedgwick saying how strange and hypocritical it seemed that any Christian pastor should accept slavery as an ordinance supported by Holy Scripture. It also shocked her that, like so many white people when talking to coloured folk, he should "jump the present life as of no account" and "furnish them with all requisite conveniences for the next".

Soon after they arrived, Pierce Butler opened the door leading from his dressing-room to her bedroom saying: "The midwife Rosa wants to make your acquaintance." "Oh! Massa!" shrieked fat, old Rosa, on catching sight of the new mistress; "where you get this lilly alabaster baby?" Fanny says herself, "I suppose if I should walk arm-in-arm with the dingiest mulatto through the streets of Philadelphia no one could possibly tell by my complexion I was not his sister". To Rosa, however, she appeared almost divine, and, indeed, to most of the other coloured people too. Margery the nurse also came in for much admiration, and the baby girls were accorded a kind of worship.

The letters written at this time to Elizabeth Sedgwick enable us to see precisely how Fanny was affected by her new surroundings. They go into every detail of slave life; the management of the estate; the accommodation; the hospital treatment; the nature of the work; the provision for old age—nothing material is omitted from the survey. Being written by an Englishwoman with no experience of Southern life the letters display horror and guilt at being even remotely responsible for so great a crime against society. Even Miss Sedgwick, New Englander though she was, could not share the English girl's resentment. After all was said and done, she was well accustomed to the idea of slavery, and too loyal to the Union to dare to be an abolitionist.

After considering the possibility of reforming her vassals, Fanny decided that a desire for cleanliness must somehow be impressed on these poor, dirty people. There seemed no great harm in offering a cent for clean faces and heads, and another cent for clean hands and feet; later, perhaps, when willing co-operation had been won, it might be possible to deal with the body. Meanwhile it was better to hasten slowly. The response to her suggestion was immediate. If "Missis" will but give soap "we will be so clean for ever", promised eager tongues. This easy success prompted her to deal with the dirty babies of women working in the fields. What could be done for them? Their mothers went out too early to wash them and returned too weary for anything except to throw themselves down and sleep. Could the elder children in whose charge they were left be paid for washing them, or would that be undermining the mothers' self respect? Self respect? had they got any to be undermined? Fanny wondered.

There was so much to investigate, and investigation was welcomed. Never had the negroes had an enthusiastic, energetic young white woman troubling about them before. What might not be achieved through her help or intercession? When it was found out that

"Missis" meant to see the cabins in which they lived there was quite a flutter. "Missis" must see everything; the living-room, the sleeping closets, the rude bed-steads heaped with grey moss, the pestilential-looking blankets. To swift inquiries they responded; Yes, there certainly were two families of, perhaps, eight or ten persons in each hut. Stuffy? Well, they had not bothered about that. The huts themselves, as Fanny saw, were just wooden frames pinned to the earth by a brick chimney, with ducks and chickens walking in and out, as it might be in Ireland. No chairs, tables, plates, knives, or forks were to be seen. How did they eat? That was easily answered. Men and women sat on door-steps and scooped their mash out of cedar tubs or an iron pot. One or two owned a broken metal spoon dis-carded by the manager, but most used pieces of wood, and all children their fingers. How very near they were to animals, thought Fanny, as she watched boys and girls rolling, playing, tumbling about in the dust like puppies, or else lolling with half-shut eyes against walls in the sun.

Fanny began her house reforms by telling the hands to clean out their cabins, tidy them up, and light a fire on the hearth. As they did not seem to understand what she meant, she began to illustrate her wishes. Surprised to see a white person use her hands, they imitated wonderingly. Having initiated this good work, she walked down the little avenue of cabins to the infirmary, a building of four rooms set in two stories. Courage was needed to penetrate into this abode of

dust and vermin, but Fanny had never been afraid of
anything. Half the casements were glazed and so dirty
that no more light came through them than through
the unglazed openings with dark shutters closed. Sick
women lay or sat on the floor or on settles. There was
no bed, mattress, or pillow to be seen, nothing but
tattered, filthy blankets, and oh! the stench! It is better
to give her own words: "I stood in the midst of them
unable to speak, tears pouring from my eyes at the sad
spectacle of their misery. Some of the women were ill
with fever, some were in childbirth, some set fast with
rheumatism." She ordered old Rosa, who was in
charge, to let in light and tidy up. Then she proceeded
herself to make a fire. Rosa objected: "Let alone, Missis,
let be; what for you lift wood? you have nigger enough,
Missis, to do it". From the women's ward she went to
that of the men and found conditions there just as bad.
What a shame it all was, what a crying shame! Surely
Pierce could not know; she would go straight to him
and the overseer and tell them about it. "Covered with
dust and vermin," she approached the office. The overseer, who had only been a few months at Butler's
Island, explained that when he first came he felt reforms were needed, but that when the former manager
told him that the hospital had been in that condition
for nineteen years he could only assume the owners to
be indifferent to the welfare of their slaves and, therefore, had taken no steps to improve it. Pierce promised
that something should be done.

Worse things, however, were to come to Fanny's

knowledge. She was sick with disgust when she found that one of the slaves, Harriet, who had told her that a woman working on the plantation had no time to keep a baby clean, had been flogged for having said this. At dinner one day the overseer told Pierce Butler that another hand, Chloe, had been flogged for "cheek". He then proceeded to talk casually of other things; flogging was all in the day's work. "My dinner tasted bitter in my mouth," wrote Fanny to Elizabeth Sedgwick.

Obviously there was nothing to be gained by tackling two men together on the subject of punishment; she would wait and have it out with Pierce. In any event it was better to know the worst, to understand the system on which the plantation was worked, than to bang away in the dark as it were. About this flogging business, for example, it seemed to be an understood thing that all the negroes working at Butler's Island should be subject to the head-driver, Frank, who divided the labourers into gangs, each in charge of a "driver" furnished with the leather thong of authority. Each of these drivers could inflict, at his own discretion, one dozen lashes. If the slave still proved refractory he then had to report to the overseer or head-driver, who could order fifty lashes, the limit of punishment allowed on this estate by Major Pierce Butler, Pierce's grandfather.

For nineteen years this estate had been profitably worked for the benefit of absentee landlords, and the manager had saved enough money himself to buy a place in Alabama for his middle age. The Butlers were so well satisfied with his administration of the property that Pierce thought he deserved a good present from the family. With this idea in his head he bestowed on him "Joe", husband of Psyche, the nursery maid, and father of her two children. Fanny was horrified when she discovered his intention. "Joe" raved at Pierce Butler and threatened to kill himself. With folded arms his master told him not to make a fuss over what was inevitable. Psyche was in despair, and Fanny implored her husband not to commit so great a cruelty. The clamour was such that, though Pierce refused to withdraw his offer, Mr. King was forced to say that it did not suit him to receive an unwilling present.

The whole system of "managing" slaves was abhorrent to Fanny, and the more she knew the worse it seemed. A maximum amount of work had somehow to be dragged out of lazy, shiftless, indifferent human beings who had no personal interest whatever in the tasks they were set to do for the term of their natural lives. What incentive could there be to work hard if the work had no end and benefited neither them nor their children, even though they had toiled for thirty or forty years? Of necessity the whip was the only argument that held, for since you could not deprive them of their corn mash or their kennels, and they had nothing to lose in the way of property, no other form of compulsion could serve the master's end. For the most part slaves were not afraid to die, indeed many of them welcomed death as deliverance, but they did fear suffering, and suffering was hanging like a sword of Damocles always above their heads.

Fanny felt that it was revolting to all decency and self-respect that her young and strong husband, on being petitioned by what in plantation lingo were called "lusty" women to lighten their work in the fields, should lecture them on malingering and bid them work as before. She could not command her feelings sufficiently to stand by during the interview. Was it possible, she wondered, to keep any respect for a man after so unmanly an exercise of authority? The older "hands" all told Fanny how considerate Major Butler had been in former days and how the manager had dehumanized the administration of the estate.

When the gentlefolk, for any reason, abandoned their plantations to live elsewhere, abuses incidental to absentee landlordism sprang up as surely in Georgia as in Roscommon. There is no doubt that many negroes lived happily under the kindly, patriarchal rule of Southern gentlemen who did not have to screw a living out of them, but could afford to give in to their lazy ways and dilatory habits. Major Pierce Butler had been loved by his hands. One day he had assembled "the force" in order to present a certain slave with a silver goblet engraved with an inscription commemorating his gallantry in saving life. As an example of the kind of attachment inspired by a good master, it is enough to state that the goblet is still a cherished and unbuyable possession in the family of that slave.

Things were no longer the same. The estate was run

on a purely commercial basis, and the treatment of the hands was almost mechanical in its absence of human sympathy. At least that is the way it appeared to Fanny, who was constantly brought up short with irritation at injustices or cruelties. In her more sober moments she did not put the blame on her husband, for the system obviously was not his fault, but he irritated her the whole time by his apparent acquiescence in the arrangements of the manager. There was nothing of the reformer about him; he took the line of least resistance and seemed to enjoy plantation life.

Religious instruction, for some reason, was not encouraged by the manager. One evening a young negro came to the house to request permission to be baptized. Pierce curtly refused that permission, to Fanny's disgust. What could one think of a man who could act in that way?

Fanny held one or two religious gatherings herself on Sundays, using a Church of England Prayer-book, a hymnal, and an *Imitation of Christ*, borrowed from Margery. These few meetings made her feel nearer to her flock, but they did not endear her to the estate manager.

Tender hearts were rare on Butler's Island, and soon Fanny was occupied from morning till night listening to petitions and entreaties. "By their unpaid labour I live; their nakedness clothes me, their toil maintains me in luxurious idleness," wrote Fanny to Miss Sedgwick, with a pattern sentence in her head. The real agony of mind lay in the growing suspicion that her presence was making things worse for the slaves. True that beds, mattresses, pillows, and clean blankets had been provided for the infirmary, that babies were competitively washed and freed from their stinking red flannels, that boys and girls soaped their faces. Such concessions improved all relations on the estate, but Fanny found that the limit of the influence was reached when she petitioned for any indulgence that absolved a slave from rendering the maximum amount of work. Pierce Butler told her no negro could be believed on any subject, and that she should know better than to listen to their nonsense. The application of this principle was made clear by "Teresa", who told her that she was to be flogged for having complained that her health did not permit of long turns in the fields. With a pang Fanny realized that it was owing to her talk with her husband that this infamy was to be enacted. Bouncing into his office she accused him of cruelty and made what is called "a scene". He maintained there was no hardship, no injustice; that "Teresa" had not done her task by the appointed hour and, as a matter of routine, had been ordered so many stripes. The mere fact of his wife being at Butler's Island could not be allowed to upset the whole system of discipline on the estate. Back flashed Fanny on the brutality of allowing a man to strip and lash a woman, the mother of ten children, and to exact from her heavy toil in order to maintain himself and his brother in luxury; and what were they indeed but two idle young men who happened to be owners of the plantation! Surely if he had a spark of manliness or humanity the whole business of managership must be abhorrent to him. He admitted it was disagreeable, and the interview closed with disgust on her part and irritation on his. "God knows," she wrote to Miss Sedgwick, "when I married Mr. Butler I knew nothing of these dreadful possessions of his!"

The talk of the negroes as she wandered about among the cabins distressed her. It was hateful to have a woman say, "Look, Missis! little niggers for you and Massa; plenty little niggers for you and little Missis". But then, there was no aspect of slavery that was not hateful.

For anyone who had literally coined money by her own exertions it was an extraordinary experience. Never had she reflected when so gaily and generously she gave up her earnings to her father what the humiliation was to be of being maintained by the unpaid labour of slaves.

An excursion to outlying huts at Woodville and the residence of Hammersmith, standing in the pine barrens where Major Butler had once lived, gave an idea of the size of the property, and the return in a board-cart drawn by "six cows and bulls through deep sand, like a Merovingian monarch", made her laugh. After all, she was young and strong and there was much to enjoy in this green, beautiful place with all its variety of scene and scent. One day she rowed over to Darien town lying on its bed of sand with side-walks shaded by magnificent live oaks twisted and trimmed into grotesque forms by the sea winds. She struggled

FANNY KEMBLE

Aged 23

From a portrait by Thomas Sully.

Reproduced by courtesy of the Museum of Fine Arts, Boston, Mass.

through the deep sand of the road to call on the doctor's wife. The doctor, a shrewd, intelligent man, was often severely tried by Fanny's diatribes against slavery. He pinned his faith for the future on Mr. Clay, "a man on whom slave-holders could depend". His wife from New England had what Fanny called "the dearly beloved snuffle of the Berkshires", and was a kind, pleasant woman. It seemed odd to pay calls in this remote place, but it was obligatory, and another day she went with Pierce to return the visit of Doctor Tunno, whose island-home was surrounded by gardenia trees of incredible size.

The days brought their burden of joy or sorrow. One day Shadrach, a valuable slave, caught pneumonia, and, in spite of careful nursing by Pierce and the doctor, snuffed out suddenly like a candle. "They have no stamina, these corn-fed people," commented the manager. Fanny, deeply moved, provided the winding sheet and went with her husband to the funeral in the evening. The coffin lay on trestles outside the cabin; hymns were sung and prayers said kneeling. Mr. Butler stood and Fanny knelt in the dust. The negro Loudon spoke of Lazarus and the hope held out by his resurrection. The ceremony concluded with the invocation of a blessing on Mr. and Mrs. Butler and their children. The irony of it! Fanny wept as she walked behind the coffin to the grave half-full of water. "God bless you, Missis, don't cry," said a voice from out the circle of torch-bearers as Mr. and Mrs. Butler walked home silently by the dykes in the blue night.

Yet another estate, famed as a long staple cotton-growing district, formed part of the property—St. Simons. It had to be visited, and Pierce Butler went ahead to make arrangements for the family to stay there. Fanny, alone at meals with the squinting, slow-speaking overseer, probed deeply into the problems of slavery. He was thankful that very, very few of the slaves could read or write, as every childish step in the direction of education made acquiescence in present conditions unlikely. Question after question was fired at him. Yes, it was true most women were grandmothers at thirty. No, it was not likely that English people could do a day's work on two meals of corn and hominy, but the slaves got plenty of beef at Christmas. Yes, the clothes, they were ugly and coarse enough, but he was used to them and to the niggers' dirty rags. But what about those intolerable "plains" supplied to the hands? asked Fanny; it was more like blue drugget than dress material. Well, it had always been doled out a few yards a year and two pairs of shoes for each hand; it was the custom. Was any encouragement given them to be clean or to take pride in their appearance? No, but that was quite unnecessary; and, after all, they did trade chickens and moss at Darien and buy calicoes to make up finery for themselves for Sundays; and then they sometimes danced in the infirmary. Things were not so bad when one got used to them. Coming from London it must all seem very odd, but then people from London rarely came and settled in the South.

The overseer was probably very glad when Pierce

returned to remove his inquisitive, meddling wife to the cotton estate. One fine morning the great oar-driven barge set forth with the Butler family for St. Simon's Island, fifteen miles away. Piled with beds and bedding, pots, pans, maids and children, the barge was pushed out from land. The last words of Cooper Loudon, the preacher, were a request for Bibles and prayer-books. Pierce Butler steered the course "all in the blue unclouded weather", and the negroes sang as they pulled the heavy sweeps. Their landing was announced to the people at Hampton Point by conch blasts.

As her husband led the way to their quarters in a decaying, draughty frame house, Fanny's eyes danced with delight to see its setting of jonquils, evergreen oaks, and peach trees in flower. It was a contrast to Butler's Island, which was all swamp, whereas St. Simons was all sand. Loveliness and decay, the extra-ordinary wealth of Nature and the squalor and poverty of man, were contrasted everywhere. With one glance you might enjoy a gardenia tree in flower, in another recoil from the sight of a verminous cripple. Rumour had preceded Fanny, and all babies were bonnetless, everybody had washed faces and hands, all were dressed up to file into the house and shake hands with the new "Missis". What a lot of mulattoes, thought Fanny, and how like they are to the paragon overseer who had run the estate for nineteen years!

The old, the young, and the feeble were kept for work in the cotton plantation rather than in the rice field. Here were old crones ready to gossip of past days, of Mr. King's cruelties, and of more recent happenings, such as the flogging of a negro for allowing his wife to be baptized. Conditions appeared worse to Fanny than on Butler's Island, for every natural right seemed taken away from these poor, patient creatures. Pierce Butler, having been told by the squinting overseer of the rice estate that in his opinion Mrs. Butler's presence on the property was a menace to "the institution", once and for all told Fanny that he declined to listen to any petition or tale of hers about any slave at St. Simon's. "Why do you believe such trash?" he asked. "Don't you know, the niggers are all d—d liars?" The people had done very well in the past without such advocacy, and he would have none of it. There must be a clear understanding between them; she must never speak to him on such matters. Writing of this interview to Miss Sedgwick, she says: "I was not born among slaves, and cannot bear to live among them". Since nothing she could do would help the slaves, Fanny determined she would study their lives, listen to their stories, and, by entering into their miseries, would learn "this dreary lesson of human suffering to the end".

Plenty of pitiful tales were poured into her ears; scars were shown; ruined bodies were exhibited before her compassionate eyes. Sights were sights, not lies or inventions, and some of the sights made her sick. The stories of Driver Bran tying women up by the wrists to beam or branch, feet barely touching ground, clothes turned up over heads and flogging them himself or ordering some deputy to do so, were an offence to language; she could hardly bring herself to write to Miss Sedgwick about such things. If the mood seized him to be amusing, it would be father, husband, or lover who would be ordered to wield the leathern thong. As Fanny listened to the sickening narrative she held the table before her so hard in order not to cry that her fingers "ought to have left a mark on it". "I should consider my own throat and those of my children well cut if some night the people were to take it into their heads to clear off scores in that fashion."

The desperate patience of the people was heartrending. Women came and entreated her as a mother to get them four weeks' exemption from field work after childbirth instead of three. She could only shake her head and "wish the sea would swallow up and melt in its salt waves the whole of this accursed property of ours. . . . Wash my soul, oh sea, and the souls of those I love from the blood of this our kind." There seemed to be no end to the suffering. Gruesome stories were told her of Five Pound Swamp, a punishment place full of snakes into which women who refused to comply with the overseers' desires were driven after flogging. "We do anything to give our pore flesh rest from whip," moaned one woman on being asked why she did not resist the overseers. Five Pound Swamp was a place of almost nameless terror.

Ever since the estate had ceased to be residential it had ceased to be human. Already the great days were over. The ruined mansion inhabited by the overseer and his wife had once been Major Butler's home. Another crumbled house had been the residence of General Oglethorpe, and an old withered tree was pointed out to Fanny as "Oglethorpe's Oak".

In the evenings Fanny maintained touch with civilization by dressing for supper. The one sitting-room was bare except for a chintz-covered couch, a deal dining-table with a baize cloth, and a few chairs. To men and women without chairs or tables it seemed a queenly apartment, and as she sat writing by candle-light the door of the great barn-like room was opened stealthily, dark figures stole in on naked feet so quietly that the boards did not creak. Men and women squatted round the hearth in the blaze of the pine logs, twelve or fourteen perhaps, showing white teeth and the whites of their eyes and staring at the figure framed in the candle-light. The evening dress excited wonder and admiration no less than the rapid and continuous writing. Sometimes Fanny took no notice, sometimes she looked up with a "Well, what do you want?" and all sprang to their feet with a "me come say ha-do" and filed out "noiselessly like a procession of sable dreams".

It was an unutterably solitary experience. She writes of visits to hospitals, of slinking home blind with tears amid curtains of scented yellow jasmine, of choking with indignation and grief while binding the wounds of some sufferer. Death was less dreadful than life. One day in the infirmary she came upon a slave, an old negro, Friday, lying on a handful of straw with a few sticks under his head and the flies gathering round his mouth. "There he lay—the worn-out slave, whose life had been spent in unrequited labour for me and mine—panting out the last breath of his wretched existence like some forsaken, overworked, wearied-out beast of burden." She bent over him with tears of unavailing pity. There was a sudden quivering, and he was free. Thank God! she said.

"I am afraid the horror of slavery," she wrote to Miss Sedgwick, "with which I came down to the South, the general theoretic abhorrence of an English woman for it, has gained through the intensity it has acquired, a morbid character of mere desire to be delivered from her own share of it."

A wall of separation seemed to grow up between Fanny and Pierce. Nothing could ever be the same after this experience. The frail bonds of passion slackened, nothing of respect or friendship or mutual interest took their place. Pierce Butler found his wife impossible as the part-owner of slaves, and registered many vows that never again should she set foot in Darien. She, being English, brooded over the character of a man who did not find it revolting to live on the work of slaves. Had he no pride? no kindness? no pity? Could it be right that he should have the power of life and death over these poor women, for it was the women certainly who were the worst sufferers. It was an utterly tragic situation, and sounded depths which no stage wisdom could fathom.

In April the whole party left the plantation for

Philadelphia. Fanny was never allowed to return to Georgia, and all Pierce Butler's future journeys were made in company with his brother. After this winter things must have gone badly at Butler Place. Fanny speaks of loneliness, of a favourite horse, "Forester", sold by Pierce to a livery man, of her publication of a book of poems to redeem him. Scattered through her memoirs are complaints that married women cannot be "independent", that is to say, cannot hold earned or inherited fortunes, "a gross injustice" which in some States of the Union has been put right. In London she told Charles Greville that her marriage had been a mistake. She found she had married an ignorant, violent-tempered man as unsuited to her as she was to him. Aware that she had outlived his love as he had outlived her respect, she feared "lest their alienation should at last mount to such a height that living together may become impossible", and she might be "separated from her children, for whom alone she desires to exist".

A Scotsman watched her one evening at a performance of *La Sonnambula* in Philadelphia. A small figure "with eyes full of latent fire" sat beside her husband and seemed engrossed in the performance. In the last scene she rose and threw a wreath at the feet of the *prima donna*. "I wondered", wrote the discerning tourist, "if she did not regret leaving the stage to pine like 'a dull weed on Lethe's wharf' in the midst of the most unappreciating of all communities."

HARRIET MARTINEAU

HARRIET MARTINEAU

§ I

A LADY was sauntering in the Zoological Gardens of Liverpool one Friday afternoon in August 1834. Her eyes turned ever and anon to the weathercocks above the houses. Was the wind going to drop, or would she have to pass Sunday without a change of clothes? It was unthinkable that she should wear her "sea-dress" at any church, and yet it was almost as unthinkable that she should pass a Sabbath without attending divine worship. Books and needlework were packed; she was indeed bereft of consolations. Early Sunday morning word came to her that the captain of the *United States* had hired a steam tug to tow his ship out to sea. The lady, accompanied by a meek female companion, drove to the dock in high feather. "Have you no misgivings?" asked an intimate friend. "None," replied the adventurer, who had determined to relish every moment of impending enjoyment.

Stepping aboard the New York packet this English spinster waved good-bye to her escort, watched till there was nothing more to watch, and then pranced along the deck to arrange her cabin. Unpacking pens, reams of writing paper, a pocket Shakespeare, and "a little black silk cap without which no lady should put to sea", she arranged her possessions for a six weeks' voyage. Deep in her box lay letters of introduction from everyone who mattered in London—letters from Lord Brougham, Mr. Hallam, Mr. Rogers, Lord Durham, Miss Mitford, Miss Aikin, Lord Althorp, Mr. Macready, Mr. Malthus. Never had any female crossed the sea armed with such compelling weapons for forcing doors. Like all assured celebrities she was gracious and even-tempered, and the discovery that she was a good sailor added to her innate sense of superiority. Other passengers might lie about retching and groaning in cabins, but Harriet Martineau, "lashed to the binnacle", enjoyed the buoyancy of the ship as it tossed amidst "the green restless mountains" that she admired so much.

Without exaggeration, Harriet Martineau may be set down as the perfect traveller. The disposition to admire her extravagantly for being able to eat anything and sleep anywhere is mitigated by the discovery that she could neither taste nor smell. Likewise the condolences which would naturally flow towards a gentlewoman dependent on an ear-trumpet for communicating with her fellow creatures are stemmed by finding that she looked upon it as a positive advantage, ensuring as it did the undivided attention of great men and undisturbed private conversations on prickly subjects like nullification and slavery.

Accompanying the authoress was a person discreetly and usually alluded to as "my friend" and in less guarded moments as "Louisa J." Miss Jeffery, a subaltern soul, supplementing as it were the ears, the eyes, and the memory of her employer, seems to have had but a faint individual life, though creating a pleasant impression of gentility on those with whom she came in contact. Twenty-one other passengers were on board, ceremonious introductions were made by the captain, and some quite young men told Miss Martineau that they thought no more of crossing the Atlantic than a Cockney would of making an expedition to Primrose Hill. Statements of this kind were rather surprising to one who had never left England before.

At the time when this voyage of observation was undertaken Harriet Martineau had wrung a career for herself out of the most unpromising circumstances and was, if not the best, one of the best-known women in England. Of Huguenot stock, and daughter of a Nor-wich manufacturer of bombazines and camlet who gave his eight children a good education but was unable to endow them with money, Harriet early de-veloped a passion for writing. *The Monthly Repository*, a small Unitarian magazine edited by a Unitarian preacher, W. J. Fox, found its way into their Unitarian home and appeared to her the natural channel for communication with the outer world. For this periodi-cal she wrote articles and was paid for them, not in money, but in the editor's criticism and advice. At twenty, *Devotional Exercises*, by "a Lady", was pub-lished at Norwich. It gained sufficient success to have a sequel in *Addresses, Prayers, and Hymns*. Though "a Lady" might deal with religion, the same motive that impelled Miss Evans and the Miss Brontës to

adopt masculine pseudonyms caused Harriet Martineau
to write as "Discipulus" when it came to criticising
books or advocating higher education for girls. *Tracts,
Sabbath Musings, The Hope of the Hebrews,* and a
stream of similar works followed. Though nervous
and delicate, she acquired, by means of writing, a firm
foothold on the rock of life and managed somehow
to make her chief bodily handicap, deafness, subordinate
to her purpose. "My deafness when new was the upper-
most thing in my mind day and night." Somehow she
triumphed over it, and gloried like St. Paul in her
infirmity. In *A Letter to the Deaf* she appealed to
fellow-sufferers to insist upon a frank recognition of
their state, and begged them to acquiesce with patience
in all the deprivations and mortifications which the loss
of a sense must bring. Submission was no help, she was
quite definite about that; hearty acquiescence alone
brings forth cheerfulness. The ready agreement to profit by pain (emphatically a joy with which no stranger
intermeddleth!) is of the essence of triumph. "We must
be as wise as possible under a great disability, and as
happy as possible under a great privation."

Some people require to be reassured of their value
in the world; they are haunted by the sense that they
do not count, that it does not really matter whether they
are alive or dead. Harriet Martineau in girlhood misprized
her worth, but when her father died, and she and her
mother had to earn their own living at fine needlework,
she developed, in the long hours of application, a resolution to wring a livelihood and a name out of author-

ship. In spite of delicacy, deafness and nervousness, she had immense driving force, and determined at the age of twenty-seven to compete for prizes offered by the Central Unitarian Association for the best essays presenting the doctrines of Unitarianism to Catholic, Jew, and Mahommedan. The relative difficulty of presentment may be gauged by the prizes offered, ten, fifteen, and twenty pounds respectively. Under three pseudonyms and three handwritings she sent in her papers and sat down to write *Five Years of Youth* while waiting for results. When it was announced at the May meeting of 1831 that Miss Harriet Martineau of Norwich had won all three prizes and that the three essays would be published forthwith, one heart was greatly elated. With the money gained she went to stay with her brother James, a Unitarian pastor in Dublin; with the confidence gained she began to sketch out a series of small books designed to illustrate various aspects of the Production, Distribution, and Consumption of Wealth. The idea was not altogether original, for she had read Mrs. Marcet's *Conversations on Political Economy*. Study of *The Wealth of Nations* convinced her that she should endeavour to bring the doctrines of Political Economy home to the masses of her fellow countrymen, since she, more clearly than most people, saw that the miseries under which English society groaned were caused directly or indirectly by mischievous laws. Such, for example, as the Corn Laws, Primogeniture, and Penal Colonisation.

Publishers to whom she wrote unfolding her plan

declined to consider the proposition, and pleaded the Reform Bill and the cholera as excuses for their lack of interest. Knowing that interviews often succeed where letters fail she betook herself to London to stay with a cousin next door to Whitbread's towering brewery house in the City Road, and began on foggy November days to trudge four miles to the West End to market her wares. When the brewery clock boomed midnight a trembling hand was still pushing pen over paper that at least one story might be complete should luck suddenly change. Walking back one evening from Dalston she felt faint, leant against some dirty Shoreditch palings, and found herself staring at a bed of frost-bitten cabbages. Setting her teeth she said to herself, "My book will do yet". That same night she sat down to write the Preface to the *Illustrations of Political Economy.* "We propose to show," wrote the tired little hand, "what Labour can effect . . . to treat of Capital, its nature and operation . . . to exhibit the Union of these two mighty agents of Production. Under the second head, Distribution, occur the great questions of Rent, Profits, Wages, and Population, modes of Interchange, Monopolies. . . . Under the third head, Consumption, are considered the modes of Demand and Supply and of Taxation. . . . We will do our best. . . . It is our design to affix to each volume a summary of the principles of Political Economy which it contains. In this volume only we shall prefix it, in order to lead the reader to a full understanding of the purpose of this work as he advances with it." The pen was laid down, the tired hand went to the aching head, and as the brewery clock struck two "we" broke down. "I could not go to bed. I thought of my conscious power, of the multitudes who needed my work. I cried for two hours with feet on the fender and went to bed at four."

Browbeaten at length by publishers she made an agreement with Charles Fox, brother of her friend W. J. Fox, the Unitarian minister, to publish the series by subscription, a hateful job which put the full responsibility for financing the project upon her. It was agreed that a trial volume, containing the Preface to the series and the first tale, *Life in the Wilds*, was to be proceeded with at once. Reluctantly, Harriet sent out circulars to Members of Parliament, clergy, and relations. As the day of publication drew near, the publisher's letters became most disagreeable to receive. Would the author be pleased to remember that the edition arranged for was fifteen hundred copies and but five hundred were subscribed for? Miss Martineau must really make greater efforts to dispose of her work. The little paper-covered volume made a modest appearance in February 1832, and ten days later the author was entreated by Charles Fox "to hurry up" with any corrections she might wish to make, as a second edition of five thousand was to be printed immediately. She was with her mother at Norwich when this news reached her. "I walked up and down the grass-plot in the garden feeling that my cares were over. And so they were. From that hour I never had any further anxiety about employment." As the first volume was a success, she was committed to produce twenty-three others at monthly intervals; in other words, she pledged herself to write from thirty thousand to fifty thousand words a month for two years. The prospect delighted her.

From being "that deaf little woman in Norwich", as Lord Brougham once called her, she became a public character, a magnetic personality. Letters streamed in her direction: the postman gave up carrying them, they had to be fetched in a wheelbarrow. Independence at last was attainable, and after publishing eight more tales she moved from her mother's house at Norwich to rooms in London kept by a former servant. She was thirty years old, as the world counts time, when she made her entry into London society, but in November 1832 a new Harriet Martineau was born. The diffident, nervous, shy and awkward girl became in a wink of the eye the competent, self-reliant, one might almost say self-satisfied, woman who met statesmen and authors on equal terms. Happy, long mornings were spent working on the top floor of a house in Conduit Street, happy afternoons in receiving visitors, happy evenings in strolls by the Serpentine. The exhilaration of success changed as it were every cell in her body; she developed physical strength, triumph in deafness, animation of manner, sense of personal importance.

The subjects and settings of her *Tales* were varied and brought her into contact with all sorts of people. It was essential for her to be in London, within easy reach of libraries and people. Her first tale, *Life in the Wilds*, on the nature of wealth and the relations between capital and labour, is set in South Africa; local colour is laboriously dragged in by horned snakes and lions that "couch" in the vicinity. *Cinnamon and Pearls*, a later story, with Ceylon as its setting, has far more actuality, since Sir Alexander Johnstone, an ex-Governor, furnished her with descriptions of experiences in that island. Imagination was not part of Harriet's equipment, and often she had great difficulty in grinding out plots and dialogue. One story, *Berkeley the Banker*, spread over three numbers and ended luridly with the hanging of Edgar, the forger of banknotes. *Vanderput & Snoek*, dealing with bills of exchange, had Holland for a background, and the realistic setting was supplied by a retired British Consul. *Demerara* discussed and pictured slavery in British Guiana. *Weal and Woe in Garveloch* expounded the doctrines of Malthus, and subjected the author to a vicious attack in the *Quarterly Review* as a perverter of marriage. Miss Martineau was constantly asked to introduce new themes into her series. The Manchester operatives, desiring to interest her in the question of machinery and wages, sent her documents enabling her to write *A Manchester Strike*. Other people clamoured to have their pet hobbies pushed. "Flax-Growing in Guiana", "The Navigable Rivers of Ireland", "Systems of Education", were all suggested as suitable subjects for her pen.

The volumes themselves, as they appeared, made new friends for their author. Coleridge would confess, when she went to see him at Highgate, that he watched keenly for their publication. Robert Owen called on her after reading her anti-Socialist story, *For Each and for All*, one of the poorest of the series, a painful, scamped little product dealing with high life above and below stairs. The Duchess of Kent subscribed for the *Tales*, and Princess Victoria enjoyed reading them. Lord Durham told Harriet that one evening when he was talking to the Duchess at Kensington Palace, Princess Victoria came running from an inner room to show her mother the advertisement of the *Taxation Tales*. This further series was undertaken at the instance of the Chancellor of the Exchequer, Lord Althorp, who sent his private secretary, Mr. Drummond (author of the world-famous phrase "property has its duties as well as its rights"), to supply Miss Martineau with information to enable her to prepare the public for the forthcoming Budget. The chairman of the Royal Commission on Excise Taxes, Sir Henry Parnell, gave Miss Martineau the minutes of the evidence taken, together with a draft of the Report of the Committee (before they were formally presented to the Ministers of the Crown), in order that she might use the facts to pave the way for the reception of the report in the House of Commons and by the people at large. With this help she wrote *The Jerseyman Meeting*, *The Jerseyman Parting*, and *The Loom and the Lugger*. In order to obtain a background for the last of these tales she spent two days at Beachy Head, and was so much inspired by the experience that in spite of the jolting of the coach she wrote on her knees all the way to London.

Lord Brougham, the Lord Chancellor, apostle of universal education and popular literature, extolled her work extravagantly and was one of the first to realise what important services she could be made to render. He desired the Whig candidate at Norwich to engage Miss Martineau to illustrate the Poor Laws in aid of the commission appointed to examine them. Six tales were begged for on this subject, but Harriet Martineau refused to write more than four, and even these four meant overwork, as they had to be written concurrently with the *Illustrations of Political Economy*. Lord Brougham called personally to arrange terms with the writer and offered £100 for each story, £75 of which was to come from the "Society for the Diffusion of Useful Knowledge", and £25 from himself. "I never saw anything of his share of this, though I believe he was reminded of it while I was in America," wrote Miss Martineau in her autobiography. "I never made application for it, as I never esteemed or liked him, or relished being implicated in business with him after the first flutter was over." It was of course fluttering and flattering to be called on by the Lord Chancellor and asked for help, and no young woman from Norwich or elsewhere could feel anything but excited by the event.

Louis Philippe bought the *Illustrations* as they appeared, read them aloud to his family, and ordered M. Guizot to have them translated for use in the French national schools. The Czar of Russia did the same, but

Harriet Martineau's popularity with crowned heads was short-lived: the King of the French barred her books for opinions, expressed in *French Wines and Politics*, on "the assumed sanctity of royalty", for accusing his father of "inflaming popular violence for selfish ends", and alluding to him as "Egalité". The Czar was so shocked by *The Charmed Sea*, in which exiled Poles figure as working in a silver mine by Lake Baikal, that he ordered every copy of Harriet Martineau's works to be burnt and forbade her entrance to his Empire.

In *Briery Creek*, one of the *Illustrations*, she indulged her life-long hero worship of Priestley, and was rather taken aback, while staying at the time of its appearance at Lambton Castle, to have Lady Durham ask her who Priestley was.

Her daily work was carried on between half-past seven in the morning and two o'clock in the afternoon. She says that after she had mastered her thesis and determined on its setting, the story went easily. "I did it as I write letters, never altering the expression as it came forth from my brain." The manuscript bears out this statement: it is hastily written on both sides of quarto sheets of paper and full of contracted words. It was her conviction that moods and feelings had no influence on composition except in so far as it might take a quarter of an hour to get engrossed in one's work on one day and on another it would take less than two minutes. Great inequality and weakness is shown in her earlier writings, but by dint of unremitting exertion she at long last beat out a serviceable, fluent, virile style of her own that was in after years turned to good purpose in leaders for the *Daily News*, in the *History of England*, and the *History of the Thirty Years' Peace*.

The only literary acquaintance Harriet had when she first came to London was Miss Lucy Aikin, niece of the family friend Mrs. Barbauld. Miss Aikin lived at Hampstead, was intimate with the Hallams, and knew every Unitarian of note in both hemispheres. Gratified by Harriet's success she wrote to her dear friend Dr. Channing at Boston: "I paused to welcome Harriet Martineau with all her blushing honours thick upon her. The Chancellor has sent for her expressly to write tales illustrative of pauperism, and has supplied her for the purpose with an immense mass of documents accessible only to official persons. I believe she will do much good: her motives and principles are pure and high, and success, as I predicted, has improved, not spoiled her. . . . I dined yesterday in the company of Harriet Martineau and Mr. Malthus: they are great friends and allies."

So great a success as Harriet's drew notice from the world. Curious honours, such as the Fellowship of the Jennerian Society, were bestowed upon her, and she found herself submitting with something very like alacrity to being what was then termed "the fashion". In other words, she dined out and went to evening parties every day. Soon there was no spare time in her life: the days were regularly spaced. She worked till two; from two to four she received visitors; from four to six she walked. Sydney Smith, when people complained that she never returned a call, told her she should hire a carriage and engage an inferior authoress to go round in it to drop the cards.

Friendships grew like mushrooms: in less than a year she was known and well liked by the Grotes, Macaulay, Milman, Rogers, Chantrey, Miss Mitford, Miss Edgeworth, as well as by people she had less in common with, the Leveson-Gowers and the Durhams. It is tempting to add Babbage and Bulwer and other names to the list, because each name calls up some achievement and helps to reconstitute a vanished and brilliant society. In its dim candle-lighted reception rooms, Harriet Martineau, the provincial, learnt to take, and take easily, a place as a woman of affairs. The rubber tube with its cup-like end was tossed from hand to hand at parties, deafness became a kind of game, owing to the charming manners of those she met, and she enjoyed her celebrity and social success to the utmost. "She has gone through such a season as no girl before ever knew," commented Sydney Smith. "She has kept her own mind, her own manners and her own voice. She is safe." Simple week-ends spent at Haileybury College with Mr. and Mrs. Malthus, or with less famous friends at Wimbledon and Hampstead, served to rest her body, if not her brain.

Almost at the end of her task of producing thirty-four volumes in thirty months she began to think of taking a holiday. Discussing her project with Lord Henley one evening at Lady Mary Shepherd's she said Italy tempted her as the land of "sweet do nothing".

At once he begged her to think of America. "However inferior the Americans are in other respects", and he spoke into the rubber tube with great earnestness, "they have got at principles of justice and mercy in their treatment of the least happy classes of society which we would do well to understand. Will you not go and tell us what they are?" This surprising yet attractive request, combined with her own common-sense conviction that it is easier for a deaf person to hear a language she knows well than a language she knows imperfectly, decided her to take a rest in the New World. Talks with Americans in Miss Aikin's drawing-room cemented the project. Dr. Joseph Tuckerman of Boston, who was at that time immersed in the study of the English Poor Law, Representative Phillips, and Dr. Dewey all convinced her of the importance of understanding the great democracy towards which all European societies must in time approximate. Writing to announce Miss Martineau's voyage to Dr. Channing, Miss Aikin said that since Harriet was herself of dissenting parentage and connection, "she will be fully prepared to find warm hearts under cold manners, but even our sauciest travellers bear ample testimony to the hospitality they find among you".

Two days before leaving London for Liverpool Harriet was working on her last tale, *The Scholars of Arneside*. After writing the word "End" to this story, she ran into St. James's Park to enjoy her first freedom for two and a half years. It felt like flying. Grass, trees, sky appeared different from anything she had ever known. Care-free and easy in mind she returned home to pack. She had earned her holiday, and nothing in the way of annoyance, discomfort, or ill-temper was allowed to intèrfere with the enjoyment of it. Determination and robust positiveness had been cultivated in this insignificant looking woman by struggle crowned with success, and her spirit was now something that many a general would envy, for she had learnt to dominate circumstances. Some people when travelling are irritated or embarrassed by the lack of what they are accustomed to at home, but Harriet Martineau's serenity never deserted her even on the most tiresome journeys. She did not object when on Lake Huron to sharing a cabin with a fat man, their bunks separated by a white counterpane fastened with four forks; breakfasts of hung beef and strong milkless tea were eaten with enjoyment; and beds which other travellers professed to find verminous were calmly slept in.

§ II

When the pilot came on board at Sandy Hook he threw down a bundle of newspapers for the amusement of the passengers, and at once engaged in serious conversation with the Captain. Miss Jeffery was called in to the conference. She had to admit that Miss Martineau was opposed to slavery on principle, but she was discreet enough not to mention *Demerara*. The Captain, to some extent reassured, allowed the ladies to land in a tug. It was raining pitilessly; everybody had been huddled into the cabin, when a voice suddenly asked how Miss Martineau liked America, a question that was to be repeated almost daily for two years.

On landing they drove down "disappointing" Broadway to a boarding-house where rooms had been reserved. Miss Martineau was not best pleased to find families with children of all ages living under these conditions. It seemed a strangely undomestic way of going on. General Mason, a fellow guest, presided over the table at which she sat and introduced her to the Americans present. How absurd it was, she reflected, as she looked out of her window, to say that New York was at all like England. Why, in the yard below was a locust-tree, a wood-pile, two negroes at a pump, and a third negro with a large basket of musk melons! The whole scene was as foreign as could be.

It was a hot September day, and the ladies rushed out to see what they could before callers should begin to arrive. Again the "sea-dresses" proved themselves unsuitable for land wear, and the ladies perspired unbecomingly. Owing to the privilege extended to Miss Martineau of having her boxes excused the Customs they had remained on the ship, and she found she could not obtain possession of them during the week-end. An uncontrollable wish to go to church on Sunday to hear preaching and "do what others were doing" forced her into borrowing a muslin dress and bonnet from a fellow boarder. Accompanied by "Louisa J." she tripped off to Mr. Ware's chapel in Chamber Street. A well-known Unitarian minister from Philadelphia preached, in a voice she had never heard equalled for "music and volume". "I looked at my friend in much delight." Word having reached the preacher that Miss Martineau, the famed English Unitarian, was in church, the moment the service was over he wended his way down from the pulpit, greeted the newcomer with emotion, and requested her to accept the hospitality of his house if she should visit Philadelphia. Later this chance meeting ripened into an almost family intimacy, and gave lasting pleasure to Dr. and Mrs. Furness as well as to Harriet Martineau. In the afternoon many visitors came, and she "received" polite Americans until late in the evening. Robert Sedgwick called, bearing from his sister a warm invitation to visit Stockbridge immediately. Tall, bald Count Albert Gallatin came and, despite his toothless condition, entertained her with his comments on the English Court, in which he had found George IV. "a cypher" and William IV. "silly", and passed on to discourse on "the philosophy of the presidentship". . . . "While he was talking, I felt as if he was furnishing me with new powers of observation. When he was gone I hastened to secure what he had told me."

After a flying visit to Patterson and the Passaic Falls, the ladies made arrangements to go up the Hudson with the least possible delay as the weather was so hot. Recognising Edward Livingston, the Secretary of State, as a fellow passenger on the steamer, Miss Martineau promptly accosted him, and told him she had a letter of introduction to him at the bottom of her box. They had a delightfully friendly talk, and he pointed out to her Washington Irving's cottage and the spot where André was hanged. West Point seemed a lovely haven, and the nook scooped out of the rocky bank of the river and known as Kosciuszko's Garden, was especially attractive. Here Kosciuszko sat with his thoughts, and here Miss Martineau sat with hers. How enviable, she reflected, was the lot of these young students, with their beautiful lecture-rooms and library and playgrounds. The cadets by their conversation impressed her with their good manners and intelligence. The wonderful situation of the cemetery situated on a green hill projecting into the river, the monumental pillar erected by cadets to a comrade killed by an explosion, the few tombs with their simple inscriptions, and the wide-spreading trees made this spot a peaceful place for meditation. Thirty miles above West Point was Hyde Park. Its owner, Doctor Hosack, received every celebrity who landed in America, and himself was known for having been Hamilton's second in the fatal duel with Aaron Burr, as well as for being a leading physician in New York and the author of the *Life of de Witt Clinton*. With the greatest courtesy, he had asked a clergyman from New York to escort Miss Martineau to his home, which stood on a natural terrace well above the Hudson. He was an amateur farmer and gardener, and two pleasant days were spent driving about in his gig. Farming being one of the many subjects she had written on, she made an intelligent listener.

From the Hudson the travellers made their way to

Stockbridge. It was but a fortnight since they had landed. Miss Catharine Sedgwick, writing in anticipation of their visit, told Miss Mitford that she was delighted to owe to her the right to ask this distinguished lady to visit her in the Berkshires. "She has been received in New York with a cordiality befitting her claims," she continued; "to tell the truth our good people have been so roughly handled by some of our English friends that they are now a little shy of them, and an individual must have special merit to counteract the general impression." Miss Martineau was able to counteract it and turned out to be a perfectly delightful guest, simple, unassuming, and lovable. She describes herself as "exquisitely happy and the cause of jubilee to her hosts".

They talked of Miss Mitford, Miss Aikin, and Mr. Van Buren, who had been acting Minister in London until the Senate decided not to ratify his appointment. Harriet was anxious to get to know him; he shared her strong prejudice against Brougham, and there were many things she would like to discuss with him. Miss Sedgwick knew him, and gave her a letter of introduction to leave on him at Albany. In return Miss Martineau was able to tell her the talk that had been set afoot in London by his dismissal, and how at the Queen's drawing-room Mr. Van Buren had been greeted by Lord Palmerston with the information that an official *communiqué* from Washington had apprised him of the action of the Senate in his regard. He was well liked, for several people had heard the Duke of Sussex say: "What is this, Mr. Van Buren, that I read in the papers? I hope it is not true?" The King also had been heard on the same occasion warmly inviting the American diplomat to Windsor.

At Albany, Mr. Van Buren and his son called on Miss Martineau at her hotel and the Vice-President made himself most agreeable. He was a person of considerable importance in the political world, but Harriet Martineau looked at the little man with his light hair and blue eyes and could discern nothing remarkable or interesting about him. He interjected many questions into the tube but gave no information in return, and was promptly written down in Miss Martineau's diary as "a kind-hearted man" whose "manners want the frankness which denotes good breeding".

Speaking generally, she received an almost unfailing impression of patience, amiability, and lack of irritability from people casually met. Everyone showed a desire to explain everything from the beginning, should she evince the slightest desire to know. At first, possibly owing to her deafness, she found difficulty in attending to these lectures, but ended by absorbing gratefully all information tendered. In America she discerned a cold and not a cheerful spirit—perhaps the spirit of endurance would be the better word—a spirit that made the best of the stranded stage-coach, the grounded paddle steamer, the disgusting food, and the bad weather. The general absence of censoriousness, and the general wish to be fair, as well as the absence of grumbling, are all as true to-day as when Miss Martineau first remarked on them. She "basked", as modern visitors do, "in good will". The Americans have a faculty of making the best of a bad job, and they have another faculty of making the most of what is good and turning a blind eye to the evil. This pleasing quality has sometimes the defect that it destroys criticism, and adulterates true enthusiasm.

Harriet Martineau was surprised to find little real interest in politics among the people she met, but though she noted apathy about voting, she also noted considerable eagerness to influence and to pull strings, and this rather for the sake of a personal power than from any other motive. Public questions aroused no comment other than the choice of officials—and this in itself was an affair of wire-pulling—and the Americans seemed to her like the old lady who did not care what revolutions broke out as long as she had her roast chicken and her little game of cards. Though the future might be clouded by the apathy that partly at least is an inevitable attribute of the system of government by separate States, she felt sure that the country must have a bright ultimate destiny. Its size and its material resources alone ensured that.

In the conversation of the people she met she found a tendency to length and literalness, variations of old anecdotes told as new stories, much solemn pedantry, and ridiculous rhetoric. Americans not only had a disconcerting gift of narration but would listen in turn to almost any outpour. She heard a lecturer, for example, discoursing on ladies, ending a section of his address by saying: "What is the chief characteristic of women? Curiosity. Who were last at the Cross? The ladies. Who were first at the Sepulchre? The ladies."

§ III

An old intention which she carried out with great expedition was the pilgrimage to the grave of Priestley, the discoverer of oxygen. She had already made him the hero of her tale, *Briery Park*, and she regarded him as *the* Unitarian martyr. No one ever seems to care much for the martyrs to other people's opinions. Harriet Martineau was no exception, and held that to suffer for religious convictions that she herself believed to be very truth was the noblest of all experiences. From 1786 onwards Priestley had issued an annual defence of Unitarianism, and had advocated complete toleration of Papists. He liked Franklin and was intimate with Burke; indeed his unpopularity in England was secured by his letters to Burke vindicating the principles of the French Revolution. On the 14th of July, 1791, the Constitutional Society of Birmingham celebrated the fall of the Bastille. "Gunpowder Priestley", as he was by that time called, did not attend, but sat at home with his wife playing backgammon. A mob surrounded his house, destroying his papers, books, and scientific apparatus, burned his church, and actually sought his life. The Priestleys were completely taken by surprise and could make no resistance. George III., writing to his Home Secretary, Dundas, expressed himself pleased "that Priestley was the sufferer". The victim, however, was compensated to the tune of £2000, and decided to take refuge in America, where he imagined and hoped that there would be more liberty of opinion. In Northumberland, the village in which he had made his home, Harriet Martineau found a clean inn, a hostess who could give her plenty of information and who spoke with becoming admiration of her hero. Ensconced in the Priestley home were a judge and his lady, who showed her the waistcoat the philosopher had scorched with his burning glass, the balustraded roof on which he meditated in the evening, and the willows of his garden. Harriet's journey had indeed been well rewarded. As a disciple of this great man, she planted a rose upon his grave, and for another English admirer she "carried homage by planting a snowberry". This congenial place made her so happy that she remained there several days, getting to know Priestley's grandson, who was a cashier in a bank, and collecting many details of the life of this distinguished Unitarian for the benefit of admirers in England.

To so bright and curious a mind as that of Harriet Martineau everything was acceptable. Unkind people said she absorbed all sorts of rubbish and make-believe stories, but there is very little evidence of this in her books. Occasionally she is wrong about some fact connected with the winnowing of rice or the employment of slaves, but on the whole her narrative, her opinions, and her deductions ring true and sound. Her tendency was to make hasty notes; some of which bear an amazing resemblance to the casual observations of present-day travellers. In the *Retrospect of Western Life* she bunched together comments on cemeteries, mountains, slavery and the like, but on the whole succeeds in giving a perspicacious account of the things that interested her. She travelled ten thousand miles in the United States and enjoyed every moment of it till she began to interfere, during the last months of her stay, with one of the peculiar institutions of the country—slavery. Caught in the Abolitionist tide in Boston, she found "lafayetting" to cease, and got to know what unpopularity and ostracism meant.

From Northumberland she went to Philadelphia to stay with Dr. and Mrs. Furness. English people generally liked Philadelphia; for one thing they were very hospitably treated, and for another the society there was cultivated and pleasant. Everyone hastened to call on Miss Martineau, "Biddles and all". Someone had evidently impressed on her that "the Biddles" were exclusive. Society was rigidly divided up, but how was a stranger to know that? "To my great surprise I found that some of the beautiful ladies neither did nor would know other equally beautiful ladies of my acquaintance. . . . Some . . . lived in Chestnut Street, some in Arch Street. Arch Street families had made their own fortunes, whereas Chestnut Street owed theirs to their grandfathers. There was a new fashion of curtseying, the ladies of Arch rose twice on their toes before curtseying, the ladies of Chestnut thrice."

A carriage with two horses and a black coachman was placed at her disposal; "packs of cards" were left on her, and she went to endless parties under the chaperonage of her host and hostess, both extremely popular people. Harriet Martineau soon made the discovery that it was not considered quite the right thing for clergymen to go to parties. She was asked at one house whether her clerical friend had not left when the dancing had begun. "No, there he is," replied Harriet. "Oh, I concluded that he went away when dancing began," said the lady in a disapproving tone of voice. Someone else said he could not be a truly religious man since he had escorted his English guest to so many parties. Clergymen at this time never entered the theatre, and were expected to leave the company when card-playing began. "This ascetic proscription of amusements extends to the clergy throughout the country; and includes the whole of the religious world of New England."

Dr. Furness, who was about the same age as Harriet, shared her admiration for German literature. He had made translations of poems and hymns, and was at this time engaged in putting together for publication his *Remarks on the Four Gospels*. Though much perturbed by the slave question and eager to discuss it in all its bearings with Harriet, he did not identify himself with the Abolition movement till some years later, when he had the common experience of all who advocated manumission, and lost all his popularity and influence.

HARRIET MARTINEAU
From a portrait by R. Evans
Reproduced by courtesy of the National Portrait Gallery

Everyone warned Miss Martineau not to travel in the Southern States, for everyone had read *Demerara*. This tale was like a stone around her neck, but a lesser pebble which also weighed her down was a chance remark of her own which foolish Louisa had repeated to a Philadelphian lady. It was to the effect that if a black man married a white woman she "did not think Miss Martineau would interfere". Tackled with this remark she said, "I should think it no business of mine to interfere on account of complexion". "Then you are an Amalgamationist," screeched the lady to whom she spoke.

Miss Martineau's rather literal mind was genuinely puzzled, for wherever she went she saw mulattoes. What on earth was the difference, she wondered, between marriage and amalgamation as universally practised? Why should people profess to be shocked at the universal custom? Louisa, however, was rapped over the knuckles for her tactless quotation, and told not to get her friend into scrapes. Louisa meekly explained that she had been so cross-examined and cornered over Harriet's opinions that she had not known how to defend herself and so had blurted out what she believed to be the truth.

At Baltimore further warnings were given of the danger for the writer of *Demerara* to venture into slaveland. Feeling in this city was easily excited. Miss Edgeworth, whose novels were "adored" in other parts of America, was denounced in Baltimore as "a woman of no intelligence or delicacy"—because in *Belinda* she had married coloured Juba to an English farmer's daughter. One morning Harriet spread out the map and indicated to Louisa her proposed route through the Southern States, at the same time emphasising the fact that her anti-slavery views were well known and that there was to be no escort. "Now, Louisa," she said, "does it not look awful? If you have the slightest fear say so now, and we will change our route." "Not the slightest, and if you are not afraid I am not," replied the faithful companion.

A few hours' stay in Washington convinced Miss Martineau that it was clearly no place for persons of domestic tastes, but she settled down happily enough in Mrs. Peyton's boarding-house on Pennsylvania Avenue with Louisa, a Senator from Maine, and Representative and Mrs. Stephen Phillips from Massachusetts. They did everything together, and it really was great fun. The climate bothered her more than a little. One day she was muffled in furs sitting over the fender, and the next she would be out of doors in a light shawl. Her lodging was but a short walk from the Capitol, and all mornings were spent in the Senate, Supreme Court, or House of Representatives. She was shocked by the frivolity of the women in the Capitol: "I *wished* they could have understood the gravity of such an assembly and shown it some respect".

As much as possible she avoided being indoors, as the stream of callers was unending. Six hundred persons left cards the day after she arrived, and the autograph-hunters were particularly persistent. One day she was sitting in the gallery of the House surrounded by a crowd of such as thought they derived importance from her company. They talked loud to make her hear. The doorkeeper came in and told her to make less noise. She held the tube in his direction and, to her surprise, heard the man say, "You needn't put that thing to your ear; you make noise enough without it".

She sent out her cards and fifty letters of introduction the day after she had settled in at Mrs. Peyton's. The English Minister, Mr. Vaughan, was the first to wait on her, and when Congressman Phillips took her to the Senate Chamber, Mr. Vaughan introduced her to the Assembly, and later on the same day to the President. Ladies offering to call with their carriages at her lodgings to help her make her calls of ceremony were astonished to hear that these formalities had been waived, and that the President's ladies and the Secretaries' wives had already called on her. Such distinctions at once made her the "Ton".

When callers entered her parlour they found her sitting in the corner of a horse-hair sofa holding the rubber tube to her ear as calmly and unconcernedly as could be, saying sweetly as she rose to hand the ivory cup to each newcomer, "Do you know the use of this?"

There was no one in Washington save Mrs. Seaton and her mother who had read any of Miss Martineau's works. Even modish, up-to-date Mrs. Tayloe confessed that she would really have to ask "what were her novels, and if they were pretty". The gentlemen of the capital were at first disposed to laugh at the idea of a woman writing a series of books on political economy, though no one of them had the least notion of the nature of her work.

Harriet was invited to dinner by the President, the Attorney-General, the Secretary for the Treasury and by other members of the Government, not to mention the British Minister, and was bidden to many evening parties at Legations and private houses. In gatherings of strangers there was often trouble over the tube; one person would apply the wrong end to his lips, another would keep the cup pressed so tightly to the mouth that he could not pronounce a syllable. Mrs. Randolph, usually so careless of her appearance, was handsomely dressed in honour of the English celebrity, but was so scared of the tube that all her ideas were put to flight. Lovely, elegant Mrs. Coolidge was much cleverer, and conversed with ease and fluency into the mouthpiece. But whatever happened in the way of contretemps, Miss Martineau remained calm, and filled up all gaps in the conversation by talking in an interesting manner of Lord Brougham, Lord Durham, Lord Althorp, and other political personages. Of Lord Durham she said: "He will soon be our Premier, he will be the saviour of England". No one could fail to be impressed by her discourses on every sort of subject: the decreasing "use of ardent spirits by the poor; the substitution of opium for gin among the people in England, illustrated by anecdotes of apothecaries' boys kept constantly busy making up penny and halfpenny worths

of opium; the action of King William in promoting
the passage of the Reform Bill; the iniquities of the old
Poor Law. Conversations, as one delighted hostess said,
"rich in illustrations of manners, facts, and opinions".
Often Miss Martineau was heard to use the phrase "since
I have been employed by Government". Very intrigu-
ing the ladies thought as they demanded explanations,
which were vouchsafed with all the solemnity that propinquity to official life imparts.

Every hostess took pains to order a "particular
dinner" for the great writer. Mrs. Woodbury, wife of
the Secretary of the Treasury, had a wonderful meal in
her honour. Bouilli, boiled fish, oyster pie, and thirty
dishes of roast, including canvas-backs, pheasants,
partridges, mutton chops, turkey, ham, and the rest, to
say nothing of salsify, spinach, and cauliflower. Forms
of ice cream and shapes of blancmange and jelly concluded the dinner. Another hostess, Mrs. Forsyth, had
been rather more old-fashioned, ordering plum pud-
dings as a sweet course, because her guest of honour
was an Englishwoman. The "almost white" waiter
who attended all fashionable dinners, Henry Orr, reported that Miss Martineau's taste was very simple, and
that "she ate nothing but a little turkey and a mite
of ham".

Everyone found their guest plain and unaffected.
Mrs. Bayard Smith, herself an author, took her for a
drive to Kalorama, and was delighted to find she could
dispense with the tube while the carriage was rumbling
along. They enjoyed a most confidential talk all about

Harriet's early life, her motives for embracing literature as a pursuit, the formation of her mind, habits, and opinions. Speaking of the "lionizing" of celebrated people Miss Martineau said with what would appear to be inverted humility, "I have escaped that to my knowledge; I have never been made a show of or been run after as a lion." "Of course, I did not undeceive her," wrote guileless Mrs. Smith.

One afternoon Mrs. Smith had invited Miss Martineau and Miss Jeffery to dine at four o'clock. About an hour before the appointed time her daughter came in and told her that the English ladies had arrived and were tidying themselves in her bedroom. Mrs. Smith hurried upstairs and found them "combing their hair". They had taken off their bonnets and large capes. "You see we have complied with your request and come sociably to pass the day with you," said Miss Martineau. "We have been walking all the morning, our lodgings were too distant to return to, so we have done as those who have no carriages in England when they go to pass a social day." Mrs. Smith offered her the use of combs and brushes, but Miss Martineau, displaying the enormous pockets in her "french dress", said they were "provided with all that was necessary, and pulled out nice little silk shoes, silk stockings, a scarf for her neck, little lace mits, a gold chain, and some other jewellery, and soon, without changing her dress, was prettily equipped for dinner or evening company. We were as perfectly at ease as if old friends." Miss Martineau's toilet was soonest completed, and, while waiting for Miss Jeffery, she sat with Mrs. Smith on a sofa and handed her the tube. They were able to enjoy "a nice social chat" before they went downstairs.

Secretly, Miss Martineau took pride in the entertaining done by the British Minister, for it did England credit. However smart the balls at the Russian Legation might be, they could not really eclipse the dignified, well-run parties given by Mr. Vaughan. She dined with him several times, and had a happy feeling afterwards of having been a great success. One evening she helped to entertain the seven judges of the Supreme Court and seven great lawyers. It was "the warmest day that well could be. There is no merrier man than Mr. Webster, and Judge Story would enliven a dinner-table in Pekin."

Nothing was easier than to make fun of President Jackson's receptions. For the first time in history men attended them in plaid coats and leather belts, with wives and daughters in bonnets and shawls. Their manner of making obeisance to the President was unorthodox, and many of them stood on chairs, or even sat on mantelshelves, to stare at the company. Foreign ambassadors with their suites and the elegant ladies of Washington wandered about crowded rooms and created more interest among spectators than they had ever done before. Miss Martineau and her party went to a reception at eight o'clock. The President, with members of his Cabinet on either hand, stood in the middle of the first room ready to bow to all the women and shake hands with all the men who presented themselves. The company then drifted past the fireplace, where stood the ladies of the President's family, the Vice-President, and the Secretary of the Treasury. Then a tour was made of the Blue Room and the East Room. As soon as she could, Harriet Martineau stole back to watch the people filing past the President— farmers, storekeepers, ambassadors, mechanics, judges. Her underlip projected with disapproval at seeing no person of colour, though at the same time she had to admit to herself that she was assisting at "a very fine spectacle". No bad manners were to be observed anywhere, but then, as she reflected, there were no refreshments. Major Donaldson, the President's secretary, was extremely polite, and introduced guest after guest to the Englishwoman. She counted herself lucky to catch a glimpse of Amos Kendall, once the tutor of Henry Clay's children and now reputed to be thinker, organizer, executor, the moving spring, as it were, of the Administration. People said that Jackson's letters to his Cabinet were written by Kendall, that the report on Sunday mails was drawn up by him, that the circular letters from Washington to the newspapers of other centres were composed by him. Anyone so powerful and so elusive socially was bound to be attractive to every woman. Though only a man of middle years, his hair was perfectly white and his movements slow and deliberate.

When dining with the President she had the honour of sitting next him. Mr. Baird, the butler, had arranged crystal and plate with his usual taste. Two coloured

servants waited, and Mr. Baird recommended the dishes
and wines as he served them. The President talked a
great deal slowly and quietly,—a caged lion, who had
long given up roaring. He ate practically nothing, as
his health was very bad. His "phraseology" quickly
made his auditor realise, if she did not know it already,
that his life had not been spent among books. He struck
her as extremely tall and thin, and his stoop betokened
more weakness than naturally belonged to his years.
After dinner, in the drawing-room the ladies sang and
the President puffed at a long pipe *a la Parr*, in his
easy chair and retired to bed at nine.

It was immensely flattering to be so much in request
and to be so sumptuously entertained, but the evenings
Harriet enjoyed most were those spent at home talking
with distinguished men. All sorts of people dropped in
to see her, Senator King from Georgia, Mr. Palfrey, the
Unitarian minister, Judge Porter, John Quincy Adams,
Justice Story. To make a list of them would be to name
almost everyone of importance in Washington. Henry
Clay would come and sit upright on the sofa, snuff-box
in hand, and discourse by the hour in his own soft,
deliberate way as he fingered the finest maccaboy. Mr.
Webster, too, the Attorney-General, would call frequently, and lean back comfortably against the cushions
and tell stories and crack jokes till the seat shook with
laughter. One of his stories amused his audience
greatly. He said that during the presidential election of
1828 the harmful report had been put about among the
German voters of Pennsylvania that Adams had married

a daughter of George III. "But you could easily contradict that," exclaimed Harriet. Mr. Webster explained that it was never any use trying to catch up with a lie during an election, and that it had been countered by stating that his opponent had married two! Mr. Calhoun, the third member of the "triumvirate", "the cast-iron man", who looked to Miss Martineau "as if he had never been born", also came and doled out his close, rapid theoretical talk. "His mind", she observed, "has long since lost the power of communicating with any other. He meets men and harangues them by the fire as in the Senate. He is wrought like a piece of machinery set going vehemently by a weight, stops while you answer, and passes by what you say."

Justice Story became a trusted friend. Many letters exist to testify to his understanding of her mind. With him sometimes came a man to whom people looked with feelings little short of adoration, the aged Chief Justice John Marshall, whom Miss Martineau as a feminist was naturally disposed to revere, for throughout life he had invariably sustained the cause of women. No one dared to scoff at their claims in the presence of Marshall. He was a splendid, dignified, frank person, interested in English politics, and eager to know whether the people were not ripening for the abolition of religious establishment. After long study he had come to the conclusion that an institution so monstrous in principle and so injurious to true religion in practice could not be upheld for anything but political purposes. Miss Martineau was of opinion that the action of the Bishops in throwing out the Reform Bill had not strengthened its hold on the people of England. "I told him at the end of one evening that I was going to visit Mr. Madison. He instantly sat upright in his chair and, with beaming eyes, began to praise Mr. Madison." Madison later received the mention of Marshall's name in just the same manner. There was no doubt in Harriet's mind that the integrity and simplicity of Marshall raised him head and shoulders above the other men with whom she associated.

Daniel Webster, with his brown face, black hair, and cavernous eyes, was a far bigger man than Clay or Calhoun. Anyone could see that. At his own table he laid a finger on Miss Martineau's arm, and, speaking earnestly into the tube, said: "My dear woman, don't you go and believe me to be ambitious. No one can despise that sort of thing more than I do. I would not sacrifice one hour of my ease for all the honours and powers in the world." Henry Clay made no such protests to her, and with him her intercourse deepened to friendship, but it was John Calhoun, "with all his absurdities", that she gradually came to respect by far the most of the three.

Both Dr. Furness and Mr. Brooks of Hingham had given Miss Martineau introductory letters to John Quincy Adams. When he paid his visit he found Mr., Mrs., and Miss Webster clustered round the Englishwoman. "Miss Martineau", he noted, "is the author of *Conversations upon Political Economy*, which I have not read or seen. She is a young woman, I suppose about thirty; deaf and hearing only through an ear trumpet. Her conversation is lively and easy, and she talks politics, English and American." Mr. Adams was generally so unpleasant in his remarks about British book makers that this complimentary account may be taken to mean that Harriet Martineau did not make as disagreeable an impression on him as most of her fore-runners.

There was no doubt that Washington was a very amusing place to be in if you knew the political person-ages of the moment, but after a time listening to de-bates in the Senate palled, and as for the House of Representatives one could never hear anything there, so it was no use trying to pay attention to what was being said. Almost all the Senators and their wives had managed to obtain copies of *Demerara*, and she found it a trifle embarrassing to be cross-examined about it several times a day. Such focussing of attention on a hastily written tale made one long to escape to less populous places.

§ IV

Harriet Martineau never missed an opportunity of climbing a monument, and urged all travellers to follow her example. One could learn so much from merely looking down on places. A climb up the dome of the Capitol, for example, convinced her that the city, lying as it does in a marshy depression, was a grand mistake. "Its only attraction is its being the seat of government, and it is thought it will not long continue to be. The far western States begin to demand a more central seat for Congress." If the West thought like that a century ago what must it think now?

One fine day an excursion was made to Mount Vernon. Three carriages set out, and three of the party rode horses. After halting for dinner at Alexandria, they proceeded to the neglected estate. Paint was peeling everywhere, fences and gates were out of order, young lambs shivered in the biting wind. The beauty of the situation was tempered by desolation. How derisory, thought Harriet, that the British soldiers going past it in 1814 on their way to burn the Capitol should bare their heads in passing Washington's tomb. Later she had occasion to revise her opinion, for she found that neither officers nor men were aware of the "barbarous" nature of their errand. Orders to set fire to Capitol, Arsenal, Treasury, Dockyard, War Office, White House, Rope-walk, and Great Bridge over the Potomac were only issued after the convoy had arrived in Washington. In twenty-four hours the work of demolition was accomplished and the troops gone. Harriet learned with some surprise that the "horrible destruction" was carried out as a reprisal for the burning by American troops two years earlier of British Parliament buildings in York (Toronto).

After a month in Washington Harriet confessed to Louisa that she was tired of society and wished to move on. The ladies held a council of war in their boarding-house bedroom, and examined the map of the United States, the stage time-tables, and the vast extent of territory they proposed to cover. Each assured the other that she was not afraid of discomfort, night travelling, or irregularity of meals. Charleston, Columbia (S.C.), Augusta (Georgia), Montgomery, Mobile, and New Orleans were all on their list. They were cautioned by friends against the plunge, but Harriet had made up her mind to go, and nothing remained for decision but the route to be traversed and the day of departure. The Chief Justice advised them as to roads and stages and the manner of reaching the country houses to which they had been invited. Justice Story gave Harriet a general letter of introduction to use in case she got into difficulties, and this put it into the head of the Chief Justice to do likewise. "He could give no better proof how highly he esteems you," wrote Justice Story in a covering letter. "When I tell you that he is one of the greatest minds which America has produced, and is equally distinguished for his purity, his sterling integrity, his patriotism, his warm affections, his benevolence, and his undying veneration and enthusiasm for your sex, you will not fail to appreciate my feelings in regard to this compliment to you. There is no one on earth whose friendship I value more than his; there is no one whose praise is to me so touching and so dear. Pray keep his letter; it is the memorial of a man of eighty, still in the full possession of his glorious mind, and whose death, whenever it may happen, will cause a sensation in America, unequalled except by that of Washington." These ladies "have the fairest claim", wrote the Chief Justice in this moral letter of credit to the gentlemen of the South, "to the aid, protection, and services which their possible situation may require: they are of high worth and character, and I shall individually feel myself under obligations to any gentleman who, in the event described, shall be in any manner useful to them".

Looking back over the journey Harriet Martineau writes: "I do not remember a single difficulty". There was much fatigue, but that had been discounted. Stages often set out at midnight or 2 A.M. Men stood the knocking about worse even than women, for Southern gentlemen returning to their homes looked dreadfully haggard and nervous after ten days in a stage. Journeys were long; for example, it took nine days to drive from Richmond to Charleston. While the coachman and horses rested, Harriet Martineau lay down on anything she could find, carpet bag for pillow and cloak for covering. Her experience was that a short sleep of two to three hours in bed was more fatiguing than refreshing. The stages to her, but not to others, were enchanting vehicles. "I was very fond of these long journeys. The delightful American stages, open or closed all round at the will of the traveller, allow of everything being seen."

Their first visit was to the Virginian home of Mr. Madison. The stage took them as far as Orange Court House, and then a carriage completed the five miles of bad road to Montpelier, a typical Southern house, with a piazza sixty feet long supported by lofty pillars. Within were rooms for twenty guests. The ex-President was at that time a man of eighty-three, a little creature, wrapped in a black silk gown with a warm grey and white cap on his head, and grey worsted gloves. He complained of being deaf and of not being able to read much. Miss Martineau handed him her rubber tube and found him lively and playful enough in conversation. Every few hours she left his elbow to give him a rest, but whenever she went to the far end of the room he followed her. He had great faith in the future of America, but was almost in despair over slavery. Negroes, he told her, were breeding faster than whites, and every black girl was expected to be a mother at fifteen. Madison was interested to hear her impressions of Washington, for he himself had spent eight years at the White House. He was also eager to know by what influence the Corn Laws, so obviously injurious to all, had been kept in operation.

The war of 1812 had always been known as "Madison's War", and the old man seized the opportunity of an Englishwoman's visit to explain that he had never desired war, but had incurred it because the large majority of the people thought it necessary. He told Miss Martineau that it is the people who pay for a war that ought to decide upon it and not the rulers, who do not personally suffer by it. As helping to explain the outbreak of hostilities, or at least to account for their not being more carefully warded off, he spoke perhaps a little evasively of the personal interest which he conceived the Regent to have in the matter, since at that time the Droits of the Admiralty carried to the Crown a large share of the captured property of the enemy. Mr. Madison declared that the Crown had received no less than £1,000,000 a year for the two and a half years that the American War lasted. A pretty premium to pay a King for going to war! Miss Martineau hastened to assure him that such a taunt could never again be levelled by an antagonist, as in the present reign of William IV. it was settled that all sums accruing from the Droits of the Admiralty should be paid into the Exchequer for public purposes.

The talk was interesting. Mr. Madison knew he had been described as the tool of Napoleon in his designs against England, knew that the war was supported only by the greed and animus of Southern statesmen, and that it was unpopular in the North, where the fishermen sat idle on land and the frontiersmen feared the Indians let loose by the British. The Southerners, however, preponderated in Congress, and successive Presidents had been Virginian bred. Had communications been more rapid in those days there would probably have been no war and certainly no New Orleans victory.

On the 29th of May, 1812, while England stood aghast at the murder of her Prime Minister, a vote was taken in Congress favouring war unless England should repeal immediately her Orders in Council. There was no Government in England, five attempts were made to form one, and on the 18th of June America made her declaration of war. Two days earlier Mr. Brougham had brought forward a motion in the House of Commons for repeal of the Orders in Council. It had been carried without real opposition. Manufacturers hoped that America, on learning that this repeal antedated the declaration of war, would relinquish hostilities, but by that time appropriations had been voted and the annexation of Canada determined on. In July General Hull and his little army crossed into Canada, failed, gave up Detroit, guns, and two thousand five hundred men. Two and a half years later, a peace was drawn up in which the Orders in Council were not repealed, and ten days after it was signed fifteen hundred disciplined British soldiers were killed and wounded by Kentucky riflemen shooting from ditches on the banks of the Mississippi. A stupider war, either in its inception or its conclusion, Miss Martineau deemed it would be hard to name.

Charlottesville was the next halt on the travellers' itinerary. A late fall of snow prevented her from walking up to the Jefferson home, Monticello, but she did not miss much, for gone were the great days when Mr. Jefferson had discoursed on his library of twenty thousand volumes or had shown his treasures to visitors—letters from Cortez to the King of Spain, a poem by Piers Plowman, Piranesi's views of Rome, globes, maps, Greek vases—all had been dispersed. The beautiful University of Virginia of his design claimed her attention. With keen interest she inquired into its organization. Professors were listened to and cross-examined. They assured her that she was the first English traveller who had penetrated to its precincts. Thence they went to Richmond, the home of

Marshall, with its lovely views over the James River and its sweet-mannered, well-bred men and women.

As the stage rolled along Miss Martineau had plenty of time to note the curious red colour of the soil, the occasional blue bird, and the prevalent stone pine. A week of such trundling brought her to Branchville. There she took the train for Charleston, a distance of sixty-two miles, accomplished by a languid engine with a leaking boiler in twenty-two hours. It was very advanced to travel by railroad, but also very noisy, as the rails were laid on stone. This affected Miss Martineau very little, though it tired other people's heads. At Charleston she stayed with Doctor Gilman, a Unitarian minister, and his wife. Quite a flutter went through the place on her arrival. Six carriages belonging to families of the town were placed at her disposal. They all came every morning for orders, and she laughingly threatened to ride in the first and have the others drive in procession behind her. "The difficulty, of course, was to use them all equally. By employing one for the morning drive, and another for the afternoon drive and another for visiting, I contrived to show my friends that I was willing to avail myself of their kindness. Scarcely a morning passed that something came, a bouquet of hyacinths from Governor Hayne, a dish of marmalade, a feather fan, a basket of wafers, a little set of cambric handkerchiefs marked with complimentary devices from other admirers." A phrenologist sent her tickets for his course. Phrenology was then a most fashionable pursuit. As Harriet says: "When

Spurzheim was lecturing in the United States the great mass of society became phrenologists in one day. While Richmond and Charleston, however, were working away at the fifteen casts, Boston had passed on to another philosophy and was raving about spiritualism. Any lecturer on any subject was certain of a good audience in America."

"I had not been in the city twenty-four hours before ridiculous reports began to appear in the press of my championship of the blacks. Reported speeches were put in circulation which I had never made, and I was extremely careful not to allow anyone to introduce the subject of slavery, though hardly a few minutes passed before every man, woman, or child I might be conversing with opened the subject. The reports of my championship of the negroes arose from a circumstance which occurred the day after my arrival. Our host proposed to take us up a church steeple to view the city and its environs. The key of the church was in the guard-house, and our host said we might as well go to the guard-house and see it. We stayed there a few minutes, where a lady was preferring a charge against two negro boys for robbing a hen roost. They were proved guilty and sentenced to be flogged in the gaol yard at the other end of the city." Pitiful remarks made by Miss Martineau on this occasion were immediately construed into championship of the negro. This was all the more annoying since it was most important, in view of her intended tour, that she should not discuss slavery or be tarred with the abolitionist brush.

Her hosts, the Gilmans, simply adored her. They found her "playful", "serious", "childlike", "intellectual", an altogether enchanting companion. She dined out constantly during the fortnight she stayed with them. They awaited her return, and when she came in she would read a devotional hymn aloud and then "eye to eye" and "soul to soul" would "enchain and enchant" them till long after midnight. In every Unitarian household, Harriet Martineau found herself literally basking in approbation. Mornings were spent driving about the flat and sandy country amid planters' mansions with their evergreen woods and hedges of cherokee roses. Sometimes soldiers were paraded in her honour, and, as she halted with Mr. Calhoun, who had joined her in Charleston, he uncovered and addressed the men with "as much gravity and patriotic sentiment as if he were standing on the verge of a battlefield".

No woman traveller, she felt, was justified in evading disagreeable realities, so she went one morning to the slave market and was shocked at the jocose zeal of the auctioneer as he repeated the bids. "It was the most infernal sight I ever beheld." The first lot consisted of a woman and two children, a badly dressed mulatto, who appeared to be suffering from a perfect agony of shame and despair. Another lot was a small boy of eight, quite alone. The appearance of this little fellow was altogether too much for Miss Martineau's feelings and she left quickly to avoid tears. Mrs. Gilman turned to Miss Martineau and said cheerfully, "You know my theory. One race must be subservient to the other. I don't care which, but I do know that if the blacks had the upper hand I shouldn't mind standing on that table and being sold with two of my children." Mrs. Gilman resented this story being published—who would not? and denied its authenticity long years afterwards.

Mr. Calhoun travelled with Harriet from Charleston to rail-head at Branchville, and on their way discoursed on the proposed annexation of Texas, and even proposed that his English friend should draw up a constitution for the new State, for "it must", he said, "be annexed to the United States". Miss Martineau with great spirit disagreed with him, exclaiming, "The whole world must say it shall not be".

At Branchville she took the road again in one of the delightful American stages. It was all so unlike life in Conduit Street. You arrived at a lonely log-house for supper, bolted broiled venison and ham and gulped hot coffee, while the candles flickered on the faces of the six Presidents who smiled at you from all log-house walls. You then washed a little in cold water and put your hair under your bonnet out of the way of tumbling down, and got back into the stage to jolt on in uneasy slumber or jerky wakefulness along bad roads often bristling with tree-stumps, across rivers on scows in a darkness punctuated by torches: it was all adventurous and wonderful. And then the arrivals at silent rest-houses with slaves sleeping like dogs upon the floors of piazzas, the horn blowing that sent them scurrying to open doors and show bedrooms, the spreading by ladies of dressing-gowns upon beds, four ladies perhaps to a bed, the heavy sleep only to be disturbed too soon by the horn, the fumbling for reticules in darkness, and the climb once more into the coach and the wait for dawn. Harriet Martineau could not have enough of it.

American travellers could conceive of nothing more dismal than a pine barren on a rainy day, but the profound tranquillity was soothing to Harriet Martineau. The wheels moved noiselessly in the sand, no birds called, no insects shrilled. At the log rest-house a great fire would be blazing, gentlemen would stand yawning and stretching, ladies would cluster near the flames.

The aspect of the rich earth, full streams, pasturage, and fine trees of South Carolina was to an intelligent traveller most depressing because of the forsaken dwellings, crumbling bridges, and almost impassable roads, which showed only too plainly that the country was being abandoned to the old. The young men, she was told, found it more profitable to remove to virgin soil than to employ slaves in renewing the fertility of that already tilled. Slavery perhaps had not always been an economic anomaly, but it had obviously become one, and its doom was therefore sealed. It must be only a question of time before it, for business reasons, would be superseded. Going through the Creek Indian Territory she saw the common sight of "coffles" of slaves travelling westwards. "Sometimes we asked them whither they were bound and the answer was always the same, 'into Yellibamma'." Sometimes they were encamped under the trader's eye, washing clothes, sometimes loitering or laughing by the road. "It is usual to call them brutish, but I never saw in any brute an expression of countenance so low, so lost as in the most degraded class of negro slaves." Polite people never used the word "slave" in their house or on their estates. "My people" was a favourite euphemism, and sometimes "hands", "negroes", or "the force" were used—moreover, an endearing relation was assumed to exist between employers and employed. It had been illegal since 1808 to import negroes into America, but Miss Martineau was told, on what she believed to be good authority, that thirteen to fifteen thousand were smuggled in every year.

Near Montgomery she stayed on a plantation and shared the home life of a Southern family. Because an ounce of practice in such matters is worth a pound of theory, she took a lesson in cotton growing in a field of seven thousand acres with but one fence. The very shallow ploughs threw up a ridge which was wrought by hand into a line of little mounds. These were drilled and the seed was put in by hand. Nothing could be richer than the soil; it merely asked for the seed to be returned to it. On this and several other estates she found the ladies of the family engaged in cutting out slave clothing. More unshapely and hideous results could not be imagined. She could hardly believe when she was told that negro women were incapable of cutting out their own clothes, for they could not possibly do it worse than their employers. In conversation she soon discovered that as long as the slave remained ignorant, docile, contented, he was taken care of and spoken of with contemptuous, compassionate kindness. But the moment he showed a glimmer of natural endowment or of competing with whites he was treated quite differently. In Virginia it was a punishable offence to teach negroes to read and write. We hate those we injure, reflected Miss Martineau, but to be quite honest there was no real hatred to be discerned between white and black, and the copy-book maxim somehow failed to apply. Harriet found she did not care about coloured people herself; it was a trial to have them perpetually at one's heels or lolling up against bed-posts staring at one before one was awake, or standing or leaning behind one's chair. They had the oddest and most familiar manners, and never seemed to think themselves in the way. Custom breeds indifference, and when towards the close of her tour in the Southern States she stayed with Kentucky landowners she forgot their miseries as slaves and laughed at their drolleries as servants. Sitting out on the piazza gazing at clean turf dappled by sunlight coming through dark foliage, one would quite well believe that "the force" was extremely happy. She felt so gay that she took a lesson in rifle shooting, since "a rifle does not bounce like a musket", and the gentlemen had brought out their weapons for a few hours' sport among the squirrels. Everything was done to amuse her by her hosts; she was driven through droves of mules bred for work in Louisiana fields, and also was taken on an excursion to see the last herd of wild buffalo in Kentucky.

Staying long enough in the South to get an impression of its life she gives us visions of white piazzas, lounging figures, peacock feather bunches waved by negro children to keep away mosquitoes, iced drinks, unpunctuality, terror of abolitionists, and always in the background trains of dull, shuffling figures streeling off to work. Occasionally she watches a negress driving a plough. The woman is dressed in a long single-piece garment like a sack, her bonnet is poised at the back of her head, her face runs with sweat as her big splayed feet plod the furrows. Sometimes she talked to the overseers, sometimes to the slaves, and from both got an impression of dreary hopelessness and misery that made her sick. Scarlet and blue birds flit over dark fallows, but fail to irradiate the mental gloom.

It is not without interest to take a sample day in a plantation home. Breakfast is at seven. Wheat and corn bread, biscuits, waffles, hominy, dozens of eggs, broiled ham, beefsteak, tea, coffee, are all on the table. Liqueur and cake are handed round at eleven. Dinner is at two, and consists of soup, roast turkey, ham, broiled fowl, tongue, nondescript meat, usually pork, hominy, corn and wheat bread, potatoes, salad, radishes, pickles, ice-cream and dessert, and abundant champagne. A slave or two stand in attendance waving feather bunches. Supper, at seven, is usually eaten on the lap, and comprises tea, coffee, waffles, biscuit, hung beef, and ham. Coloured servants were officially fed on corn mash with pork once a week, but in practice ate almost anything there was about. It was extremely pleasant,

she found, this life of the piazza and barouche. Hosts
were so gay and friendly, horses so amenable, riding
such an enchantment that one forgot the background.
Harriet Martineau's conscience obliged her to remind
herself, by a visit to the negro quarters, that she was
not yet in Paradise. "Those quarters were something
between a haunt of monkeys and a dingy, dirty, brutish
dwelling-place for human beings."

At Mobile she met a cousin with a house at New
Orleans inhabited by himself or his partner as they
happened to be there or at Mobile. He offered Harriet
the loan of this cool, comfortable place, which was a
most opportune kindness. Accepting it gratefully she
drove through the woods, amid flowering shrubs and
over marsh land, to the pier to embark for New Orleans.
At Pontchartrain, they left the boat and travelled on
the new railroad five miles long which ran to the city
between acres of blue and white iris flowers. Justice
Porter of the Federal Senate, who had become a
familiar friend in Washington, welcomed them and
showed them the sights.

Hosts of callers began to arrive the moment it was
known that Miss Martineau was in town. It was the
same thing everywhere. At first it had pleased her, but
she was getting a little tired of it. In the short intervals
between calls the newly arrived Englishwomen sat in a
window watching the life of the streets, the muddy
streets, in which women in caps or veils went about
their business. It was like London or Norwich all over
again, calling, shopping, sight-seeing. There were

better things, however, to be enjoyed. Sometimes by warm gold moonlight they walked on the ramparts beneath the Pride of India trees and sniffed their fragrance. Sometimes they dallied in thickets of fig and catalpa, but wherever they went mosquitoes were an affliction. Some women tied their heads up in muslin bags, and also made sacks for arms and feet. Miss Martineau got into her prunella boots and wore gloves, but she was stung through every defence.

By dint of inquiring in book-shops Harriet discovered that the prohibition of books containing anything against slavery went curious lengths. Miss Sedgwick's novel, *The Linwoods*, was condemned on a single sentence; Mrs. Barbauld's *Evenings at Home*, containing a dialogue between master and slave, was sent back to its Northern publishers by the booksellers of New Orleans.

She tells the well-known story of Madame Lalaurie, a rich New Orleans woman living with a young third husband. Everyone talked of her, for she had recently escaped from the hands of her exasperated fellow-townsmen. Madame Lalaurie was a French Creole with two pallid, unhappy-looking daughters. It was always observed that her slaves looked singularly haggard and wretched, all save the coachman, who was sleek. She gave excellent dinners, and was so graceful and hospitable that no one questioned her humanity. When she had a party at home she would hand the remains of her glass of wine to the emaciated negro standing behind her chair, saying in a smooth audible whisper, "Here,

my friend, take this; it will do you good." One day a
lady living in a house adjoining that of Madame
Lalaurie heard a piercing shriek from the next court-
yard. She looked out and saw a little negro girl tearing
across the yard towards the house. Madame Lalaurie,
cowhide whip in hand, was in pursuit. She saw the
child run from story to story, her mistress following
till both came out at the top of the house. Seeing the
child about to jump, she shut her eyes and heard a
thud. Madame Lalaurie came down and picked the limp
body up and took it away. The lady watched on for
many hours, saw a shallow hole dug by torchlight in
the corner of the yard and the corpse placed in it and
covered with earth. An inquiry was made into the
affair, but Madame Lalaurie's household secrets were
revealed in another way. By the action of the cook, who
set light to the house, declaring it was better to be
burned than to live in hell, and the gallant and success-
ful efforts of French Creoles to extinguish the fire a
horrible sight was made manifest. The cook was found
chained within eight yards of the fireplace where
in the most sultry season sumptuous dinners had been
cooked. In the outhouse seven slaves were found with
bones coming through their skins, as well as two
skeletons poked into the ground. The slaves, wearing
iron collars with spikes, were chained and tied in con-
straining postures, some on their knees, some with
their hands above their heads. A cowhide whip stiff
with blood hung on the wall. Every morning after
breakfast it was said Madame Lalaurie made it her first

duty to lock herself in with her captives and flog them till her strength failed. Her coachman was her confidant, and directly her misdeeds became known he advised that she should drive out in her coach as usual after dinner and not come back. This audacity succeeded. She stepped into her carriage with an air; the crowd pressed round, the coachman flicked the horses to make them plunge, and off they went down the swamp road to Pontchartrain, where they bribed the skipper of a schooner to put off instantly to Mobile. The carriage went back; it was broken to pieces; even the horses were jabbed with knives. The house was gutted. "I saw the gutted house, gaping windows, and empty walls standing in a busy street." Wasn't that a sight to make a little Unitarian from Norwich think badly of Creoles? The pallid daughters were said to be living in great poverty and seclusion in one of the faubourgs. M. Lalaurie, however, had not been molested: people were sorry for him.

Miss Martineau went out to many parties at New Orleans and could not but admire the elegance of the French women she met. Of course they put on rouge and pearl powder, but who could complain of the result? It was, however, quite disgusting to see young ladies from Philadelphia trying to make themselves look French by this disagreeable means. Surely it would be better for these young persons to practise the French language than to copy the French toilette. Large parties, which are alike everywhere, leave no distinct impression on the mind. The parties of New Orleans

were exactly like those of any country town in England.
As always, the happiest and the most interesting evenings were spent at home, in talking intimately and at
length to individuals.

Perhaps Harriet Martineau was more impressed by
what she saw in the Catholic Cathedral at New Orleans
than by anything else in the city, for within its shelter-
ing walls whites and blacks met as brethren and knelt
side by side on the stone flags in adoration or fingering
rosaries in prayer. Of course she did not approve of
such superstitious practices herself; but the acknowledgement by any Christian sect of equality before God
was something to be noted, and when on inquiry she
found that the Catholic Church insisted that all slaves
should be baptized and thoroughly grounded in religion it gave her still more to think over. At the door
she was quick to observe that worshippers, as they
emerged into the sunlight, sorted themselves out in-
stinctively into two streams of differing colour. In this
great church a *Te Deum* had been sung in honour of
Jackson's victory over her compatriots, and on its
steps the tall General had submitted to being crowned
with laurel by Mrs. Edward Livingston, with whose
husband she had had so pleasant a talk on a Hudson
paddle steamship.

There is something exhilarating and moving about
historic scenes, and Harriet felt obliged to visit the
battle-ground outside the town which was called "the
native soil of Jackson's political growth". It was four
miles away. She was shown the ditch and the swamp

which bounded the field of action on two sides, and the remains of the breastwork of earth. "It was a deadly battlefield. I was shown a house on a plantation where, twelve days before the battle, the son of the proprietor was quietly dining at one o'clock, when a slave ran in and told him that some men in red coats were in the yard. The young man instantly comprehended that the British had captured the American Scouts. He bolted through the window and into a canoe and crossed the river amidst a shower of balls, seized a horse and galloped to the city. The troops, dispersed on different points, were collected by drum and bell; and between two o'clock and eleven at night the city was made ready to abide the enemy's approach."

The headquarters of both Generals were still conspicuous on the plain, and Miss Martineau was told by her guide that Sir Edward Pakenham, brother-in-law of 'Vilainton,' and a party of his officers were standing on the balcony of a house when an American gunner was ordered to take aim at them. Seeing the importance of the shot he became flurried, struck the river a mile off and was ordered to retire. He knew it was the crisis of his professional fate, and implored that he might be granted one more chance. He then hit the pillar which supported the balcony immediately under the feet of the group of officers, who hurried pell-mell into the house. Her companion quoted a verse from a well-known song:

> Jackson led to the cypress swamp:
> The ground was low and mucky;

There stood John Bull in martial pomp,
　And there stood old Kentucky.
And when so near we saw them wink,
　We thought it time to stop 'em;
Lord! it would have done your heart good,
　To see Kentuckians pop 'em.

"It makes one shudder", she writes, "to see the wide open space over which the British soldiers were compelled to march to certain destruction. Never was greater bravery shown by soldiers, never perhaps was bravery more abused by the unskilfulness of leaders. The result proves this. The British killed were nearly three thousand, the Americans had six killed and seven wounded. By all accounts General Jackson showed consummate ability throughout the brief campaign, and the British leaders imbecility no less remarkable. It is still incomprehensible to the Americans why the British did not all step ashore on the opposite side of the Mississippi and march the four miles up to the city and into it. It could have offered no defence, nor was there any impediment by the way." Thus did she repeat the tale she was told. The casualties were certainly dreadful, but the real numbers were seven hundred dead and eight hundred wounded. However, if the father of one's guide had been executed under martial law in Ireland one might expect an exaggeration of statement conformable with desire.

After ten days' exploration of New Orleans and its *faubourg americain*, the ladies set off north in company with Henry Clay's son-in-law and daughter,

Mr. and Mrs. Irwin and the Charles G. Lorings. They travelled by the river steamer *Henry Clay*. Forty cases of cholera had been reported the day they left, and a man died of it during the first night on the boat. No fuss, however, was made; the body was buried at a "wooding-place". In company with the Lorings from Boston and the Irwins the trip was even more enjoyable than she could have expected. On their way up river they walked for an hour in the streets of Natchez, but could not land at Vicksburg or Memphis on account of cholera. One night the air was damp and close and the moon dim, lightning flickered on the horizon. "It is not weather for the deck", said Miss Martineau to a friend, so, with two other gentlemen, they made up a rubber of whist. "In our well-lighted cabin the lightning poured in in streams and the thunder cracked overhead. Mrs. H. came to us and rebuked us for playing cards while it thundered, which she thought very blasphemous."

The voyage was, if possible, more enchanting than stage travelling. One progressed without fatigue in pleasant company, and, best of all, it was the month of May. The short, intense American spring transformed the landscape from grey uniformity to parti-coloured tapestry. Fairy-like, the redbud flared from the underbrush, and the white discs of the dogwood floated ethereally against the dark network of branches to which they were invisibly attached. Trees that put forth coral shoots livened the forests; the air was full of scents and the song of mating birds.

Harriet and the Irwins were bound for Smithland, at the mouth of the Cumberland river, and purposed to go thence to Nashville, the home town of President Jackson, and after that to Lexington. We catch a glimpse of her at this time through the eyes of Mr. J. F. Clarke, editor of *The Western Messenger* and Unitarian minister of Louisville. Writing to his friend Margaret Fuller, at Groton, he says: "I came to Lexington to see Miss Martineau and have had a capital time. I talked with her about four hours." They discussed Dr. and Mrs. Furness and Fanny Kemble, "who had been to see her every day during her stay in Philadelphia". Dr. Furness, it appeared, was a great admirer of Carlyle, and had converted Miss Martineau to his views. She assured Mr. Clarke it was "a great mistake to suppose her a mere utilitarian; she is preparing the people for Carlyleism, for they must be fed and clothed before they can be spiritualised". No English person can be completely indifferent to Mr. Clarke, since he was the exuberant person who, in 1840, at the age of forty, climbed to the top of Salisbury spire.

Staying with Henry Clay at Ashland was a delightful experience. Not only was the conversation good, but the walks and rides were full of enjoyment. They went through forests of sycamore of tremendous size, and lofty tapering beeches growing into thick clumps at the top. There were cheerful vistas between the grey boles, for they rose from soft turf unencumbered by jungle growths. One day the negroes came in to announce the discovery of a bee tree, and begged Massa to come and

271

help smoke it out. An ancient walnut was cut down and the bees evicted from its recesses. Harriet was stung, and Henry Clay capered about under the trees with a bee or two under his cravat and in his hair. It was impossible not to laugh at him, and the only result of the effort was half a tumbler of black honey.

In the end it was hard to leave Kentucky, and, in leaving Kentucky, to say farewell to slave-land. Six months' travelling had, however, convinced her that "not the least of the evils when a degraded and servile class exists to work is that work itself and all labour becomes despicable."

§ V

A trip from Maysville down the Ohio to Cincinnati was pure pleasure to Harriet. No town she had seen came up in beauty of setting to this city, "The Queen of the West".

"Cincinnati is a glorious place. Few things can be considered finer than the situation of this magnificent city." She grew lyrical over its pastures and woods and river-walks, vineyards, flower-gardens, and terraces. Commenting to an inhabitant on the rapidity of its development, he replied to her, "Yes, Miss Martineau, we have a new creation here. Won't you come and dabble in the mud? If the merchants of Genoa were princes, the citizens of Cincinnati are princes and prophets at once."

A proper sense of Miss Martineau's importance was shown as soon as she had ensconced herself at "The

Broadway". Many people left cards, and an English gentleman called and left a pile of new books and tickets for a concert in Mrs. Trollope's Bazaar. The first physician of the town, Dr. Drake, waited on her, as did many merchants and their ladies. Consulting Louisa, Harriet decided it was necessary to take a larger parlour in which to receive their many guests.

Dr. Drake fetched her in a carriage and showed her the sights soon after she had arrived. He was an enthusiast, who had lived in Ohio from the days when there were but a hundred persons in the State and they French. Parts of the city had within his memory been cane-brakes "infested by buffalo". It was like a fairy story, and the more he talked into the tube the more Harriet was worked up. This was the West then, and very stimulating it proved. "We should foster Western genius, encourage Western writers, patronize Western publishers, augment the number of Western leaders and create a Western heart," declaimed Dr. Drake, and to each statement Harriet nodded a delighted agreement.

She was initiated into the buckeye mystery. The people of Ohio were called "Buckeyes", and Dr. Drake believed "Buckeyes" to be superior to all God's other creatures. It was an amusing, exhilarating experience this dip into Western society. Why, people were actually discussing where the Capitol shall stand when the nation decrees the removal of the general Government beyond the mountains. Another delightful person, Mr. Nicholas Longworth, was quite sanguine that Ohio would become a wine-growing region. His splendid garden and singular varieties of cactus under glass were visited. What between sipping Mr. Longworth's wine and drinking lemonade out of buckeye bowls and using buckeye ladles and wearing buckeyes, parties were no end of a joke. Dr. Flint wrote a sonnet to the famous ear trumpet, which delighted its owner:

> Thrice precious tube! thou faithful voice conveyor,
> Through thy accomplished mistress' outward ear
> To that within,—wont other sounds to hear
> Than those of earth;—for all the Nine obey her
> Oft as she wills their promptings to rehearse
> In tale, or tract, or choice morceaux of verse:—
> Through thee quick, clear, and sweet response I win
> From more than Delphic oracle within.
> For spirits o'er the vasty deep I call
> Through thee; and Endor's witch to royal Saul
> The prophet's form not sooner brought than she
> The gifted minds of her fair isles to me.
> My heart's warm thanks to her I fain would speak,
> But words to tell their warmth are all too poor and weak.

One evening Dr. Drake talked in his inimitable way: "The pecan tree sheds its fruit at the same moment among the people of Indiana and Illinois, and the boys of the two States paddle their canoes and fish together in the Wabash. . . . We have no middle destiny. . . . We must unite to perpetuate for ever the green and growing West." So gay and entertained was Miss Martineau by all this attention that she had scant time to give to two insignificant young women, daughters of the head of the Lane Theological Seminary, who called on her and with whom she spent an evening at their home at Walnut Hills. The younger of the two, Harriet, a namesake as it chanced, was a teacher in the Western Female Institute. A little flame of a soul in a body, half its time "scarcely alive", reading *Corinne* and the life of Madame de Staël, and thinking, oh so quietly, about a visit she had paid to a plantation in Kentucky two years back. Miss Harriet Beecher had begun to earn money by writing *A Little Geography*, just as Miss Harriet Martineau had begun her career by writing *A Book of Devotions*. Tentative efforts, both of them, dimly grasping at self-expression. How is it that the author of *Demerara* struck no spark from the future writer of *Uncle Tom's Cabin?*

It was hard to leave Cincinnati, but the ladies did so at last by water and made their way to a most fashionable spa, Hot Springs, Virginia. It was a little trying to arrive dusty and travel-worn into the midst of such a spruce world of gentlemen in tall hats, glossy coats, and varnished pumps, and ladies in pink and blue dresses, charming shawls, gay head-dresses, and parasols. All guests, it was observed, lived in little separate cabins with miniature piazzas in front. The sulphur fountain was at the end of the green, and then, of course, there were the Assembly Rooms in which card-playing, dining, and dancing went on. As the haunt of fashion and a place set for amusement Hot Springs was not so very congenial to Miss Martineau. In this frivolous atmosphere she found herself gravitating more and more to her spiritual home, New England. Gallivanting

among gay people on plantations and at spas was all
very well for a while, but at heart Harriet was a serious
Nonconformist, and it was time she got back to people
leading lives of religious purpose. She knew, moreover,
that rows of hosts and hostesses were expectantly awaiting her in Boston and its vicinity. Dr. Channing, the
recognized leader of the Unitarians in Massachusetts,
had already received accounts of Miss Martineau's
qualities from his friend, Miss Aikin, and had invited
the traveller to stay with him and his wife in their
holiday home near Newport. It seemed best to Harriet
to go to Rhode Island first and to pick up, as it were,
the thread that would lead her through the labyrinth of
Bostonian life. Intercourse with and approval by the
Channings would ensure her entry into its society
under the best auspices.

Dr. Channing, a little fellow, dry and shy to begin
with, and then as his shyness wore off, amusing and
full of laughter, drove her all round the country in his
gig, "even to Purgatory". The word "Purgatories" was
somewhat curiously applied to extensive fissures in the
rocks along the seashore. He pointed out "Whitehall",
the house of Bishop Berkeley, built for him in 1729,
standing snug and grey among the trees looking over
the town, the beach, the sea. Together they walked to
the pile of rocks which was Berkeley's favourite place
for musing, and where the conversations of "The
Minute Philosopher" are supposed to have taken place.
"It was melancholy to visit these retreats and think how
empty the land still is of the philosophy he loved." In

the evenings they discussed religion and politics. Harriet Martineau discovered in discussion with him that he defined Unitarianism, not as designating the materialistic views of Priestley, but simply as anti-Trinitarianism. "The word Unitarian", he said, "includes all who believe there is no distinction of persons in God." Taking everything into consideration this was a far more edifying visit than any Harriet had paid for some time, and it was with a feeling of great confidence that she left for Boston. Writing to Miss Aikin, Dr. Channing observed that though he did not rate his guest very highly as an economist, he esteemed her "among the first moral teachers and the first writers of our time".

Dr. Joseph Tuckerman, philanthropist and missionary at large in Boston was eagerly civil to Harriet on her arrival. It interested her to learn that he, her friend Stephen Phillips, and Dr. Channing were known because of their close intimacy as the three in one. Held in equal friendship by them all was a new-comer, Charles Follen, whose liberal opinions had obliged him to leave Germany. In him Harriet Martineau was to find a twin soul. The Charles G. Lorings, with whom she had become intimate on the Mississippi voyage, the Ellis G. Lorings, the Sedgwicks, and Judge Story had all invited her to stay in their homes. Going to Boston was like going into the most delightful and appreciative family circle. Harriet felt she could pour herself out in a kind of spiritual abandonment to these understanding friends. The comfort of staying among people who thought as you thought, and who had read the *Monthly Repository* for years, and not *Demerara* only, but all her other tales, could hardly be put in words. It had to be experienced as a sensation of well-being. Harriet, like most people, was always at her best in an atmosphere of approval. It warmed her as it warmed those who generated it.

Native New England caution was set aside by her hosts as they received her with open arms, and, by reason of her own expansiveness, hearts opened all round her, and the most warm and kindly friendships resulted. "We had wintry hearts," said one of her admirers, "she melted them." First in one house then in another did she have these cosy, eminently domestic experiences. It was almost a self-indulgence to let people into the secrets of her early life. To Justice Story she confided all, and gave him a copy of her autobiography. He found the narrative deeply interesting and promised to "cherish it with peculiar pleasure as a mark of your confidence". . . . "You delighted me", he says, "by your sketches of your life and pursuits; your calamities and your noble triumph over them. I pray God to preserve you many years as a blessing to your country and to the world. Never forget that there are thousands of bosoms in America which will beat high whenever your voice speaks to them from the other side of the Atlantic. . . ." As some return he offered to show her the sketch of his life, though he feared Americans had not yet learnt the art of memoir writing.

During her stay at Boston Harriet Martineau attended the Federal Street Meeting-house of which Dr. Channing was minister. Its congregation was distinguished by social prestige and it must be remembered in speaking of Unitarianism in America that at that time it embraced much of the influence, wealth, and literary culture of New England.

We may accompany Harriet and Louisa to a Sunday morning meeting in the Federal Street Church. The doors are thronged by well-dressed men and women, all eager to reach their seats. Within there are few vacant places, but if respectable-looking strangers appear owners of pews hospitably invite them to share theirs. When the ladies have shaken out their skirts and the gentlemen have done praying into their tall hats, a person, small in stature, thin and pale, advances with rapid, elastic step up the aisle and ascends the pulpit stair. For a moment or two he looks benignantly over the congregation and then, laying aside his big coat and wraps, puts on a black silk Genevan gown, selects a hymn and a passage of Scripture and waits for the hour to strike. A voluntary on the organ is followed by an opening invocation by an assistant minister. Then Dr. Channing arises with outspread arms saying, "Let us unite in prayer". All follow his petition, then a Bible passage is read, a second hymn is sung, and the congregation settles itself for the sermon, which is generally long, attentively followed, and felt in the form of emotional and intellectual uplift. At the close another petition is put up, then the benediction

is given from the pulpit, the fashionable throng files out
to greet co-religionists on the pavement.

Maria Weston Chapman, later to become Harriet's
greatest friend, first caught sight of the renowned author
in church and noted the brown abundant hair beneath
the bonnet and the peculiar eyes, varying in colour
from grey to green and almost blue. She had already
marked her down as a recruit to be enlisted under the
abolitionist banner.

Among so many sympathetic people it is hard to
single out any for special notice, but the intimacy with
the Charles Follens was of quite an unusual character.
The Follens were living at Watertown during the
summer of 1835, and there began the friendship that
"never suffered even the common fluctuations of
friendship but which strengthened and deepened with
time and knowledge". "Our meeting with you, dear
Harriet," wrote Charles Follen, "was a blessed recognition rather than a new acquaintance." In this household she felt completely domesticated and was able to
speak out her whole mind frankly without fear of losing confidence or loosening attachment. She shared in
their simplest pleasures, and, when she could not be
with them on Christmas Eve, they deferred lighting up
the Christmas tree till Sylvester evening. Enjoyment
without her, even of the customs of the Fatherland, was
no enjoyment.

Kind, intelligent, hospitable people sprang up in her
path. It was almost embarrassing to be so much sought
after. A visit to the Stephen Phillips in their Chestnut

Street home at Salem revealed a fresh aspect of American life, that of the great Eastern merchants and the skippers in their employ. That Englishmen had no monopoly of Oriental trade as one had of insular conviction assumed was a surprising fact. Here in this New England port Harriet listened to queer seafaring tales of whale-killing in every sea, of marketing ice in India, of wild days in Mozambique. She met men who had plucked willow sprigs from Napoleon's grave, and saw in their houses strange wallpapers of Eastern design, Chinese copies of English prints, and filagree chessmen of stained ivory. It was enough to kindle the slowest imagination: the local interest of Salem witches faded as Harriet's eyes opened on the wide marine horizons such trophies evoked.

Excursions were made to Manchester, Ipswich, and Gloucester. At Manchester piles of mahogany were lying on the jetty, and cabinets were stacked ready for despatch to New Orleans. Most of the good furniture of the southern cities was derived from this neighbourhood, and the little town, distinguished by its graceful lantern tower, was prosperous. At Gloucester, which reeked of drying fish and barrelled mackerel, Harriet was presented with a huge bunch of dahlias. Mr. Phillips was a delightfully appreciative host and caused the portrait painter, Charles Osgood, who was painting members of his family at the time, to make a picture of his guest, which was afterwards hung in a very special place in his study.

§ VI

As an act of respect to Noah Webster, the father
of pacificism, Harriet visited New Brighton, where
this venerable, white-locked Unitarian lived with his
daughter, the post-mistress. His pamphlets denouncing
war had been much read in England; and Harriet was
anxious to assure him of her sympathy. Another notable
outing was made to 'the Rock' on 'Forefathers' Day'.
'Forefathers' Day' was pure joy from start to finish.
Fine snow was falling, and the icy sea was fringed with
grey ice thrown up by the action of the waves. There
was no colour anywhere, save for the few patches of
green grass that showed on Burial Hill. 'It is the great
birthday of the New England people!' exclaimed Harriet
delightedly, as she prepared to take part in the rejoic-
ings of those present. Mrs. Hemans, she reflected, had
misled her by describing the coast as rock-bound in
her lyric; as far as her eyes would reach it was low and
sandy, and there was but the one rock. And that rock,
perhaps, was not all one would wish it to be, as it had
been split and the top part placed within an iron railing
with "1620" painted on it; but still it was historically
a holy place. A congregational minister from Scotland,
visiting Plymouth in 1835, wrote: "The Rock! The
Rock! I had a feverish desire to see it!" Indeed, till he
had seen it he could settle to nothing. "You look for a
bold piece of rock-work standing out distinct and alone,
instead of which it is under your feet. . . . I stood on it
and trembled as I stood. I know of no spot more sacred

HARRIET MARTINEAU

From a portrait by Charles Osgood.

Reproduced by courtesy of the Essex Institute, Salem, Mass.

upon earth except the one spot where the Holy One suffered, 'the just for the unjust'." For many Non-conformists 'The Rock' became the symbol of conscience.

The essence of New England to the inhabitants of Old England is a distillation of strange purity. Customs, manners, and pronunciations which have disappeared in the older country give a feeling of greater antiquity to the new. Eighteenth-century English streets, completely equipped with bow-fronted, red-brick houses, porticoes, lanterned church towers, lyceums, athenaeums, and town halls, greeted Harriet Martineau as she went to and fro on her visits and excursions. Villages of charming austerity composed of white frame houses set around greens were to be found at Lexington, Concord, Wenham, and many another place. Their graceful, fountain-like elms and aloof, white, weather-boarded churches gave an impression of life unspotted by the world.

Perhaps the most appealing of all was Northampton. Here the stage was hailed by a gentleman, who asked for Miss Martineau. It was Mr. George Bancroft, the young historian. He cordially welcomed the two ladies and majestically ordered the stage to climb the hill to his house. Such a house it was, too, of spacious rooms, standing on a lofty terrace with a balcony that overlooked the garden, the orchard stretching down the slope, the sedate village, and the river with its meadows. Beyond all, in the opposite distance, rose Mount Holyoke. Far off to the left lay Hadley parsonage, the hiding-place for many years of Goffe, the regicide. Still further to the left lay Presbyterian Amherst College with red-brick buildings conspicuous on the heights.

A more delightful host than Mr. Bancroft could not be imagined. He was full of information, drove his guest to the college, where she saw everything, including the Observatory. He had spent three years at Göttingen. His library held the works of Goethe, Humboldt, Niebuhr, Mignet. He could show a first edition of *Don Juan* inscribed by its author. Above all he was interested in religion and till recently had "filled the pulpit". He told Harriet that his first meeting with his dear friend Ralph Emerson had been on the occasion when he had come to preach for him at Northampton. The last day of her visit was spent with him among the moss-grown tombs of the early settlers, the long grass of the graveyard illuminated by spikes of golden-rod.

"We expected only to admire, but she has made us all love her", wrote Catharine Sedgwick, after Harriet had paid her last visit to Stockbridge. "She has adopted American manners, eats her egg from a glass, and holds her fork in her right hand . . . she has been honoured, praised, and homaged, not to say worshipped, by the great as well as the small." The friends enjoyed delightful walks and drives together. Sometimes they went down a beautiful ravine between a mountain and the brimful Housatonic; sometimes they sat on Laurel Hill and looked down from Sacrifice Rock over green meadows, yellow wheat-fields, and white homesteads. Wherever they were they talked, possibly Harriet did most of the talking, for Catharine, after eight days of intercourse, says: "She is quite aware of her own superiority and perhaps a little too frank on this point, bordering on the dogmatical". The friendship had its small though invisible flaws, which were accentuated into cracks as circumstances changed.

At Harvard, a village between Groton and Concord, where she stayed with Mrs. John Farrar, the writer of many books and the wife of a professor at Cambridge, Harriet felt herself to be in the very heart of eclectic America. Here was nothing common or unclean. Striking up a warm friendship with a fellow-guest, Margaret Fuller, she discussed everything under the cope of heaven with her and insisted that her friends, the Ralph Waldo Emersons of Concord, should invite her dear, brilliant, new acquaintance to her house. Margaret Fuller at first thought Harriet the most enchanting and interesting woman she had ever met. It was a short-lived bedazzlement, for it was not founded on common political interests or religious experience and, like the wheat sown in shallow ground, it withered almost as soon as it had grown. Walks in Sleepy Hollow with one friend or another of that speculative Concord circle set Harriet cogitating in her mind on the spiritual values of America. Obviously the people she was living amongst were in no sense representative. But who or what really does represent America and by what shall it be judged? For example, do newspapers

express the mind of America? Harriet asked herself—
there were twenty-five for every one published in
England—or do Americans put the best of their mind
into something totally different, such as legislation,
which is of a very high order, or the organizing of new
communities and corporations? She judged them to be
an eminently imaginative people, though it was clear
to her that they did not exert their power in literature
or the arts, but rather in politics, commerce, and development. "If the American nation be judged by its
literature it may be pronounced to have no mind at all",
wrote Harriet, a little severely, as she tapped the work
of contemporary authors. Washington Irving might
perhaps beguile intervals in rough and busy lives, but
Fenimore Cooper's works had, in her opinion, a puny
vitality, and Bancroft's *History of the United States*
was little more than begun. As for Catharine Sedgwick's
novels they had a certain charm and local interest, but
there was not much to be said about them. Then, again,
the periodic literature—what was there to pit against
the *Edinburgh Review* or the *Quarterly*? Absolutely
nothing—it was all of a low order; and the American
Quarterly, published in Philadelphia, was uninteresting
because of the "triteness of its morals and a general
dearth of thought". After this survey she concluded
that it was quite an open question whether, in literature,
"Americans are capable of distinguishing a creation
from a combination".

As to what people in America read—it was indeed
a difficult question—Hannah More she had heard of

everywhere; she certainly was much better known than Shakespeare. Scott was idolized and so was Miss Edgeworth, but most of all Americans raved about Mr. Bulwer, and the man who exercised an enviable sway over thinking people was Mr. Carlyle. When *Sartor Resartus* was issued piecemeal in *Fraser's Magazine*, it was snatched at in the United States and was read eagerly when it appeared in book form, for it seemed to meet some pressing want in minds weary of cant and mechanical morals. In her more lenient moods Harriet Martineau set down in her diary that Americans were the most sweet-tempered people in the world. Perhaps it was this very quality that sapped their critical faculty.

Breaking in on these enjoyable visits, and the reflections they engendered, there sounded every now and again a faint call to action. Harriet was compelled to realize that people were looking to her for help. Maria Weston, wife of Mr. Henry Chapman and the very soul of the abolition movement in Boston, had written to Miss Martineau, when she was still in Kentucky, begging her not to be deluded by her southern hosts into acquiescence in slavery. Though she had received but a cold acknowledgement from Ashland, it in no way deflected her purpose. Extremely pretty, much admired, and unaccustomed to rebuffs, she renewed her attack on Miss Martineau in Boston. In the flesh she was irresistible. Rosebud cheeks, golden hair, blue eyes, winning smile, and great directness, all made their impression on Harriet, who listened to her as she listened to few women. People called Mrs. Chapman the Joan of

Arc of the movement. James Russell Lowell wrote of her:

> There was Maria Chapman, too,
> With her swift eyes of clear steel blue,
> The coiled-up mainspring of the Fair
> Originally everywhere.
> A noble woman, calm and apt,
> Cumaea's Sybil not more rapt,
> Who might with those fair tresses shorn
> The Maid of Orleans' casque have worn;
> Herself the Joan of our Arc
> For every shaft a shining mark.

By degrees and rather in spite of her instinct for not interfering in the affairs of another country, Harriet Martineau was drawn into the abolition movement. The ardent missionary, Mrs. Chapman, was in part responsible, but the person who finally pushed her over the brink was William Lloyd Garrison. She happened to be in Boston the very day on which he had been mobbed and dragged through the streets by a halter. Revolted by the incident Charles Follen had thrown up his tutorship at Watertown to join the Massachusetts anti-slavery society in Boston. Both he and his wife, Elizabeth Cabot, threw themselves into the movement in the most uncalculating way, and so did their friend Samuel May, another minister.

Garrison's name was familiar enough to Harriet, for it had become a household word in London during his visit there in 1833. He knew her friends Lord Brougham and Mr. Macaulay, as well as Mr. Wilberforce and other champions of the negro. He had spoken at Exeter Hall.

Sir Thomas Fowell Buxton asked him to breakfast as a means of becoming acquainted with him. When Mr. Garrison presented himself, Sir Thomas scrutinized him doubtfully and said, "Have I the pleasure of addressing Mr. Garrison of Boston in the United States?" "Yes," said Mr. Garrison, "and I am here in accordance with your invitation." Lifting up both hands Sir Thomas exclaimed: "Why, my dear sir, I thought you were a black man!"

Miss Martineau met him again and again with the Follens and found him "the most bewitching person she had ever met". He convinced her that it was unfair for her not to declare herself an abolitionist, that it was cowardly, in fact, to have published *Demerara* on the safe side of the Atlantic and refuse to testify on the unsafe side. Garrison admired her greatly and wrote a sonnet in her praise, of which the sestet runs as follows:

> To one alone I dedicate this rhyme,
>   Whose virtues with a starry lustre glow;
> Whose heart is large, whose spirit is sublime,
>   The friend of liberty, of wrong the foe.
> Long be inscribed upon the rolls of Time
>   The name, the worth, the works of Harriet Martineau.

One November day, by Charles Follen's request, she attended a meeting of the anti-slavery society held in the house of Mr. Francis Jackson. Harriet and Louisa dined first with Mr. Loring. "You will be mobbed", said Dr. Ware, as he made ready to drive them from Cambridge, where they were staying with him, to Mr. Loring's house in his "carry-all". Lovely Mrs. Chapman and the Reverend Samuel May were also of the party. "My hopes", said she, as she threw her golden hair under her bonnet, "are stronger than my fears." "Have you physical courage?" once more enquired Mr. Loring of Miss Martineau, "for you may need it now." It was a ladies' meeting, coloured females were seen going up the steps, and on the pavement boys were hooting. One hundred and thirty women were there, all of them members of the Abolition Society save Louisa and Harriet. The three gentlemen remained on guard, but within hearing in the hall.

At the close of the meeting Mr. Loring scribbled on the back of a hymn paper begging Harriet to speak a few words. It sounded a harmless request, but to comply with it would entail many penalties. Hospitable doors would close in her face, acquaintances would glare at her stonily, there would be no more comfort or pleasure in travel. All the annoyances of social ostracism would in future be her lot. She accepted the challenge and, feeling very nervous, she rose and began to speak:

" I have been requested by a friend present to say something—if only a word—to express my sympathy in the objects of this meeting. I had supposed my presence here would be understood as showing my sympathy with you. But as I am requested to speak, I will say what I have said through the whole South in every family in which I have been, that I consider slavery as inconsistent with the law of God and as incompatible with the course of His Providence. I should certainly say no less at the North than at the South concerning this utter abomination—and now I declare that in your *principles* I fully agree."

Dry, clerical little speech as it was, it caused Mrs. Chapman to bury her face in her arms with emotion. Mud was being hurled at the windows; there were hoots and yells to be heard. But somehow the ladies were driven home safely by Dr. Ware, and thus a decisive day closed.

Some three weeks after this meeting Harriet went to stay just outside the city of Boston with a "stirring preacher"—Mr. Walker of Charlestown. Here she made the disagreeable discovery that she was not to be visited. At first the absence of callers was put down to the wintry weather and the cold drive across the Charles River. Even though her friend Miss Peabody tried to keep her from reading the newspapers, Harriet soon discovered that "filthy extracts" were being reprinted from the New York into the Boston papers. The Walkers could persuade no guests to meet her. Doors banged in her face, no new ones seemed to open. It was a terribly new experience. From Boston the abuse spread. Southern newspapers with mock interviews reached her. She was "a foreign incendiary", she "should be hung" or "have her tongue cut out and cast on a dunghill". Months later she went to New York, and her host, on whose arm she entered the ballroom, was cut dead by fourteen of his acquaintances. Isolation threw her more and more into Mrs. Chapman's society and cemented a friendship which death did not close, since Mrs. Chapman was the appointed editor of her *Autobiography*.

Her real friends, of course, rallied round her. Charles Follen ceased subscribing to the *Daily Advertiser* because of its rude onslaught. Charles Emerson stood up in a manly way for freedom of opinion and freedom of speech, saying "he would rather see Boston in ashes than that Harriet Martineau or anybody else should be debarred in any way from perfectly free speech". His brother, Ralph Waldo, opened his house at Concord to her at the very height of her unpopularity. Judge Story, who had always been on the side of the angels and had known what it was when he delivered a charge to a jury denouncing the slave-trade for the newspapers to demand that he be hurled from the Bench, was always ready with understanding sympathy.

Nevertheless, the humiliation of being abused after having received homage was bitter enough to cause her to revise, even to alter, many of the estimates she had formed of the American people. And always she harped on what to her was the most noticeable and striking feature of the American spirit, its moral timidity.

Everywhere she observed this curious deference to opinion. It was something that did not exist in London. Accustomed as she was to a free critical attitude of mind Harriet was most severe about the lack of it in America, and laid down that "the worship of opinion is at this day the established religion of the United States". And again she says, "The worship of opinion certainly takes precedence of that of wealth in America. So long as men live—not for truth and justice, but to be respected and useful—civilization can never be high."

Many thoughts and comparisons had been suggested to her by her visit to Cincinnati. What was it that made New Englanders in especial so detestably cautious? They certainly appeared to her to allow themselves less liberty of speech and action than is enjoyed by the inhabitants of countries whose political servitude the Americans justly compassionate and despise.

Caution, she opined, might be a form of selfishness, but surely Americans must be unaware of its extent and singularity. It had come under her notice that they never expressed themselves freely, they never wrote good letters, they feared their falling into wrong hands. And yet what harm could the force of opinion or publicity do compared with the evil of living in perpetual caution? It is true that every man may hold office once in his life, and to do this it seems that he must not have committed indiscretions on paper or in talk, for it might be brought up against him. Americans cannot possibly conceive the easy, comfortable state of society in which no man fears his neighbours, and each man may have responsible opinions of his own. The restraint imposed by the servitude to opinion makes for a misery and a dullness without parallel. The sunshiny, bold complacency she had met with in the West made New England a little dim and tarnished and old-fashioned.

When persons suffer for their convictions they are

prone to despise and deride the easy-going people who do not complicate their lives by taking sides in any controversy. Margaret Fuller thought abolition so low and disagreeable a subject that she would not tolerate its discussion. Harriet retaliated by writing her down "a pedantic woman in a pedantic town and a pedantic age", and further stated that she was self-deluded and lived in an ideal world of most fanciful and shallow conceits which the transcendentalists of Boston took for philosophy. And all the while the liberties of the Republic were running out as fast as they could.

Catharine Sedgwick also fell from favour. One evening they had walked together arm-in-arm by "sweet Housatonic", debating slavery and its implications. Something Harriet said made Catharine snatch her arm away, exclaiming, "The dissolution of the Union! The Union is sacred and must be preserved at all costs!" Harriet had replied quietly, "The will of God is sacred too", and as she spoke an uncomfortable suspicion formed itself in her mind that, "judged by English standards", her friend fell short of truth. "She thought me rough and rash . . . she thought safety a legitimate object of pursuit and I did not." In one of her books, *Home*, Miss Sedgwick had described a family as "spending Sunday afternoon on the water after a laborious week and an attendance at public worship in the morning. Religious conversation was described as going on throughout the day." So much offence was taken at the idea of a Sunday sail that the publisher requested the author to alter the chapter, as he wished to destroy the first printing. "I am sorry to say she did alter it", comments Miss Martineau. "If she was converted to the popular superstition, which could scarcely be conceived, no more is to be said. If not, it was a matter of principle, on which she ought not to have yielded."

Other factors contributed to temper the warmth of earlier friendships. As intimacy with the Follens grew other intimacies became superfluous. Even the company of the faithful Louisa J. could be lightly dispensed with. There was no reason for her to remain in America now that Harriet had other companions closer to her spiritually and mentally than Miss Jeffery could ever hope to be, so back to England she went some months ahead of her employer.

In seclusion, as from a watch-tower, Harriet Martineau looked down on the maze of American life with special reference to the path the clergy were following in regard to emancipation. A measure of solitude is necessary to the cultivation of perception.

It had been something of a shock to get a letter from dear Dr. Furness lamenting her precipitate action at the anti-slavery meeting, and a sadness to realize that Dr. Gilman thought abolition a crime. How curious it seemed that clergy as a body should be so deeply snared in worldly toils. The Episcopalian clergy, she noticed, kept silence on the question, but such influence as they had was used in a highly conservative manner. The Unitarian ministers were not much better. With the exception of Samuel May, the first Unitarian pastor to side with the right, Charles Follen, who prayed aloud in church for "the miserable, degraded, and insulted slave in chains of iron and chains of gold", and Dr. Channing, who preached in favour of abolition, she could see no other reformers. With all her knowledge of and sympathy with clerical life, she stated it to be her belief "that the clergy were the most guilty class in the community since they profess to spend their lives in the study of moral relations and are pledged to look at all questions from the point of view of God". The slave-holding and mercantile classes had no such pretensions and were by comparison guiltless. "If the clergy of America", she said, "follow the example of other rear-guards of society, they will be the first to glory in the reformation which they have done their utmost to retard. . . ." "The fearful and disgraceful mistake about the true nature of the clerical office is the supposit:on that it consists in adapting the truth to the minds of the hearers." If she had had to epitomize the reasons for the general set against emancipation observable in the mass of the people, she would not have summed them up as economic or even selfish, but as being in essence the worship of an idol and the fear lest it be overthrown. The idol was of parchment, its name—The Act of Union. So long as men worshipped at its shrine there could be no abolition. Such was the vision of the hour, but Harriet Martineau lived to see the day when, because many hundred thousand Americans were willing to lay down their lives for this parchment idol, abolition was brought about.

§ VII

In the spring Charles and Elizabeth Follen carried Harriet off to a farm near Stockbridge, where they paid but two dollars a week for excellent food and accommodation. There they hunted marsh flowers, wood anemones, and violets. Harriet did a good deal of writing and some walking, though not nearly as much as she thought necessary to health. Walking she found was not the custom of the natives: "No American will trudge two miles if he can get a lift on a wagon". Together with the Follens she planned one last tour in which the Lorings were to be included. The first stage of their journey was Detroit, which they reached by way of Erie Canal and Lake. Thence they drove in an "exclusive extra" through the land of the Potowatomies, Indians wearing plaques of silver on their breasts, helpless and troubled by the hordes of squatters who had suddenly invaded their territory. By shocking roads they jolted on through the red summer lilies and the pink moccasin flowers till their arrival at Michigan City was heralded by horn blasts. After a night's rest they went on in and out of the sand-hills to Chicago and descended from their post-chaise to find its primitive streets crowded with land speculators. A negro in scarlet, riding a white horse and carrying a scarlet banner, announced the hours of sale. Everybody was in a state of rush and excitement very exhilarating to witness. Lots to the value of two million dollars could be had by purchasers. A man told Miss Martineau he had just paid five thousand dollars for a plot that was worth but seven hundred and fifty earlier in the day. They saw a young lawyer who was earning five hundred dollars a day in drawing up land titles. The whole scene gave an impression of intense faith in the future of America and a feeling that a new era was being inaugurated.

On the Sunday spent at Chicago the newly built, unfinished Lake Huron Hotel was the setting for a Unitarian service. Dr. Follen preached to an attentive audience sitting on boards supported by trestles.

With considerable spirit Harriet decided to return with the Follens to Detroit by sailing-vessel, while the Lorings went home by land. The navigation of the Lakes was quite a chancy business, for they had never been surveyed, and strange winds and storms and shoals were the lot of those who cruised upon their waters. Harriet and Elizabeth Follen occupied the empty ladies' cabin by night, but the rest of the ship was so congested with men returning from land sales that they had to surrender it to them as a sitting-room during the day. This boat was the only place in which Harriet was treated to bad manners by any American. The supper-table was full when they presented themselves the first evening of the voyage; no one made room for them, but a few words from the captain caused the men to be more polite. The fare was hard tack, salt pork, and tea without milk, but Harriet felt very well on that as on all other food. "The dish from which I ate was, as on other occasions according to some, mutton; to others, pork;

my own idea is that it was dog." Whatever it was, it was always disposed of with appetite.

Owing to the captain's intervention no more "gentle-men" came to the ladies' cabin to smoke, to snooze, or to spit. It was obviously unfortunate for ladies to stray into boats, for they got mixed up on hob-nobbing terms with men accustomed to the freedom of the saloon and the stable-yard.

Miss Martineau had read and profited by Mrs. Trollope's book, and she was not going to be so stupid as to repeat her criticisms. "Of tobacco and its conse-quences I will say nothing but that the practice is at too bad a pass to leave hope that anything that could be said in books would work a cure. If the floors of boarding-houses and the decks of steamboats and the carpets of the Capitol do not sicken the Americans into a reform; if the warnings of physicians are of no avail, what remains to be said? I dismiss this nauseous sub-ject." Quite sensibly she said, "No nation can pretend to judge another nation's manners".

Some of the passengers cleared off at Milwaukee when the ship lay grounded on a sand-bank, and there the ladies had the cabin scrubbed clean of tobacco juice and took complete possession. As soon as this was done, seven young women came down the companion-way, seated themselves, and began to question the voyagers. They were the total female population of Milwaukee, which had been settled eight months earlier; at that time it numbered four hundred souls, but boasted a newspaper, a printing press, and stores. "We were glad to see these ladies," observes Harriet, "for it was natural enough that the seven women should wish to behold two more when such a chance offered."

A stout gentleman, one of the proprietors of the ship, came aboard and demanded accommodation in the ladies' cabin. "We had no right to complain and helped the steward partition off the cabin with a counterpane fastened with forks." There were many pleasures to counterbalance this propinquity—watching the Wisconsin coast, the white barracks of Mackinaw against green hills, and the old French village with yellow houses and red shutters. Breakfast with the commandant on lake trout, new bread, and cream was a joy. Presently a dilemma occurred, the captain and mate both went sick, and there was no one to steer the ship up Detroit River. There was nothing for the ladies to do but to clamber out on a cargo boat and be put ashore.

A visit to the Rappite Colony below Pittsburg and a farewell visit to Dr. and Mrs. Furness in Philadelphia concluded this happy tour. On the first of August, after nearly two years' travelling, Harriet Martineau sailed from New York with a head crammed with opinions and a heart full of emotions. Packed in her box was a humming-bird's nest for her niece, secured in Fanny Kemble's garden. The Follens wept on the quay, "fearing they would never reconcile themselves to losing her". Harriet sent them from London a complete set of her *Tales*, and Charles Follen thanked her for her "beautiful present" and for her "eye-blinding love messages". "The quill", he said, "is but a poor substitute for the tube." Harriet stated in print that she thought Charles Follen "the most remarkable and the greatest man" she met in America. They were never to see each other again; he perished four years later during a coastal voyage from New York to Boston.

§ VIII

In some respects Harriet Martineau, among all English critics of the United States, was the most severe; she found there much to admire, but though impressed by the obvious prosperity she was not blinded by it. "That form of self-confidence which is commonly called conceit grows in favour with me perpetually. An overestimate of self appears to me a far less hurtful and disagreeable mistake than the idolatry of opinion." She enjoyed having Americans thump the table and talk about their confounded prosperity, and the size, the inexhaustible size, and native wealth of their country. She did not mind their throwing out their chests—that was optimistic and manly; the "puffing system"—or "boost" as it is now called—amused her mightily. But there was another side to it which she found some difficulty in expressing with accuracy. In perspective it appeared to her that American reputations were made by a group of money-making men. Garrison alone among the people she had met could have made his way against public opinion. The great men of America seemed to her, as it were, proxies for rich men who in some odd way became famous in the success of their undisclosed principles. She gives examples of what she means in Dr. Channing, who was the agreed representative of piety, though in no sense a great man; in Edward Everett, the typical gentleman and scholar; in Judge Story, the popular jurist and good fellow; in Webster, the model statesman and advocate. Each of these men was really no more than the voice, business or otherwise, of the people who had made him. They were not leaders but competent men who all seemed to her to act according to direction with no personal convictions transcending the commonplace interested ideals of the wire-pullers. It was all part and parcel of the strange moral timidity or caution which made Americans afraid of extremes. She wondered whether any great man could ever arise under such an oppression.

Her somewhat didactic book, *Society in America*, was unfavourably reviewed and regarded as a cruel breach of hospitality. She was cursed as a woman of robust health, tough nerves, and the frame of a moss-trooper, who scampered round the country in order to obtain materials to vilify it. Margaret Fuller was specially severe about the book, which, if published to-day, would be considered dull in arrangement and arbitrary in tone. "Does a woman of circumscribed education and recluse habits feel herself competent to teach a whole nation?" asked one reviewer. What particularly annoyed most readers were her comments on American food; here is a woman, they said, "who has waxed fat and kicked", feeding on American delicacies instead of "stale bread and butter, chalky milk and slop tea", which is all she would ever get at home, daring to criticize our perfect meals. It really was the height of insolence from a foreigner.

A second and more popular book, much preferred to the former by Sydney Smith and Carlyle, *A Retrospect of Western Travel*, is far more entertaining, but it is not in the least indiscreet. The line Bostonians took about both books was, "She fed at our tables and she calls dear, delightful Boston pedantic". But even in Boston should one expect to buy a traveller's opinions for a cup of tea?

Society in America made an unpleasant impression on practically everyone she had met during her tour. Dr. Channing wrote to Miss Aikin, saying "that it was in as bad odour as Mrs. Trollope's book, perhaps worse". Letters reached Miss Martineau in England filled with abusive reviews or weighted with stones on which she had to pay postage. She was accused of being "a spy", "a leveller", "a Malthusian dragon-fly", and other queer things. It was not the first time she had taken hard knocks, and this time she took them cheerfully. Missiles hurled across the Atlantic could not hurt her; vilification by post was nothing to what she had had to put up with in Boston. The books were well liked in London and gave her a claim to be recognized by all serious people as an authority on transatlantic matters. The old satisfaction that she had first known in earlier days at Norwich was re-enforced by subsequent experience, and the fact that she had extricated herself unaided from the rut of poverty and insignificance gave her great self-confidence and buoyancy of manner. She knew herself for a personage; her work was in demand; and, highest of all aims, she was serving her generation according to the light that was in her. Life, though health failed, became ever more enjoyable and richer in content. Harriet Martineau was a happy woman when she went to America, and on her return she described herself "as the happiest single woman in England".